A STUDENT'S COMPANION FOR
Patterns for College Writing

Laurie G. Kirszner
St. Joseph's University, Emerita

Stephen R. Mandell
Drexel University

bedford/st.martin's
Macmillan Learning
Boston | New York

For information, write: Bedford/St. Martin's, 75 Arlington Street, Boston, MA 02116

ISBN 978-1-319-51139-5

Library of Congress Control Number: 2023931202

Opener banner design: ©JonnyDrake/Shutterstock

CONTENTS

17 Punctuation   179

PREFACE FOR INSTRUCTORS

A Student's Companion to Patterns for College Writing reinforces the most foundational elements in academic writing. While recognizing and respecting students' abilities, this supplement breaks down the steps necessary to excel in college writing, tackling time management; critical reading skills across print, digital, and professional genres; the essay drafting process; and the essentials of grammar. This companion, meant to supplement the coverage in *Patterns for College Writing*, gives students the additional support they need to get or stay on-level in the composition classroom. It is an ideal solution for accelerated learning programs or corequisite courses, while the deep integration with *Patterns* makes it a useful resource for any instructor who wants students to build a strong foundation in academic writing.

Part 1: Academic Success

Part 1 addresses topics that are critical to student success: academic planning and time management. This coverage can be a useful way to begin the term or can act as a handy reference for students outside of class.

Part 2: Breaking Down the Patterns

Part 2 begins with step-by-step coverage of critical reading and the structure of the college essay. This discussion is followed by an expansion of each of the rhetorical modes in *Patterns for College Writing* (narration, classification and division, argument, and so on), with help for each: understanding the pattern, organizing an essay around it, and a case study that breaks down a student's writing process for that particular pattern. Students can clearly see how various assignments require different preparation and response, and the case studies model a variety of techniques for prewriting, organizing, and revising. Additionally, this section provides advice on taking good notes in class and preparing for an in-class exam (see pages 89–91).

Part 2 also introduces the concept of **TEST** (Thesis statement, Evidence, Summary statement, and Transitions), a unique memory tool that inspires student confidence and independence. This simple self-assessment tool helps students to recognize and incorporate key elements as they read and revise their own writing. Thus, **TEST** lays the groundwork for student reading and writing, preparing them to work independently to analyze their reading and empowering them to revise their writing with confidence.

Part 3: Guide to Language and Mechanics

Part 3 is a detailed grammar supplement. It provides some of the support of a handbook, including coverage on punctuation, sentence structure, and even some common spelling concerns. This quick reference material gives students context for instructor comments.

Appendix: Sample Student Papers

The appendix offers two sample student research papers and accompanying discussion questions. It provides models for students to examine as they work through their own writing, supplementing the student examples seen throughout *Patterns for College Writing*.

PART ONE

Academic Success

Academic Planning

Some studies have shown that college students rarely or never meet with an academic advisor to plan their futures.[1] That sounds like a boring detail, but it's actually meaningful.

Whether you attend a two- or a four-year school, why should you bother with academic planning? Well, think about it: You could, in theory, hop in a car and drive across the country without using GPS, following road signs and navigating by the stars. You might even make it to your destination without any major detours, but that's unlikely — and who'd want to take the risk? It's the same thing with higher education. You need a personalized road map to reach your destination; otherwise, you might end up stranded.

Academic planning is a vital step in your college career, and it should be an ongoing process that starts on day one. Once you lay a foundation for your studies, you'll save time and money, avoid missing credits, and take ownership of your education. It's no coincidence that students who engage in academic planning are more likely to stay in school than students who do not. They are the people who know where they're going and how to get there.

We'll show you how to chart your path to a better shot at success in college. And if you don't know exactly what you want to study, we'll help you find your inner compass.

1.1 The Bottom Line

Planning your classes in college is even more important than it was in high school. Think about it: You now have hundreds of choices, so you'll need to pick wisely if you want to earn your degree in a reasonable time frame. Whether you're planning to be a neuroscientist or a dancer one thing holds true: You're responsible for learning the requirements for your program *and* taking those courses in the proper sequence.

---

[1]See the Community College Survey of Student Engagement: https:///www.ccsse.org/

Dropping even one course can have important consequences. Many college courses are prerequisites for classes you'll need down the line. For instance, if you're an English major and drop a first-year composition class, you might not be able to register for upper-level literature courses. The fallout might be graduating a semester or even a year later than you planned, which could be stressful and expensive. A delayed graduation can mean the difference between earning minimum wage for several more months versus landing a well-paying job in your field.

No one expects you to figure it all out on your own. Your academic advisor is a key player in your college support system. You'll probably be assigned an advisor as soon as you enroll, so take advantage of that expert guidance. Even if registering for classes sounds easy to you, you don't want to go it alone.

Planning your college course work from the get-go saves valuable time and resources. Even if you're on financial aid, resources aren't endless. If you randomly take courses without a specific goal in mind, your tuition funds could dry up before your plan takes shape. Tuition can be expensive and there's pressure to choose a direction early. You don't want to graduate mired in debt.

If you haven't settled on a major yet, a little up-front planning can help you keep your options open. Lots of first-year students have no idea what they want to study in college; many change their minds midstream. Even with all the uncertainty, it's still essential to have a strategy. Start by building a solid base of general courses that could qualify you for a few different majors. And leave time in your schedule to explore other subjects that grab your interest. Do you like math? Try an accounting or economics class. Do you love *How to Get Away with Murder*? Sign up for Criminology 101 or the equivalent.

1.2 Getting in Gear: Your First Meeting with an Academic Advisor

Before you register for classes next semester, sit down for a strategy session with your academic advisor. On most campuses, you'll be assigned an advisor (usually an instructor or staff person in your field). Some colleges let you choose your own advisor, whereas others offer special advisory centers run by adjunct professors or retired faculty members. A good advisor can help you choose courses, decide on a major, weigh career possibilities, and map out your degree and certificate requirements. Your advisor can also recommend instructors and simplify all aspects of your academic life. You're still the captain of the ship, however. And there are a few ways to make sure that your first meeting is a valuable experience.

Strategy #1: Do some advance work. Schedule a meeting with your advisor as soon as possible — college instructors are busy, and you'll have to work around their schedule and commitments. Before you go, look at the course catalog, think about the available majors, and familiarize yourself with campus resources. If you haven't decided on a major, talk to a counselor in your career center and take an aptitude test to help you narrow down your options. The early days of college are critical; once classes start, you might not have time to do in-depth research.

What to bring to the meeting

- Your academic transcripts. Take a personal copy even if you submitted one with your application. Your school record is an important tool; it shows your academic advisor where you've been, what you're good at, and where your interests lie so that you can plot your course accordingly.

- A list of programs that appeal to you. Academic advisors love it when students come prepared — it shows that you're passionate and taking your future seriously.

- Your time frame and goals. Do you plan to enroll full time or part time? If you're at a four-year school, when do you plan to graduate and with what degree? Will you need to go on to graduate school to finish your studies? If you are at a two-year school, do you want an associate's degree or a certificate, and do you plan to transfer to a four-year college?

Strategy #2: Know the right questions to ask. Once you've chosen a major, the biggest question mark is how to move forward in your program and meet the necessary requirements. Fortunately, the process is straightforward. You have your prerequisites — the basic core courses you need to get out of the way before you can enroll in upper-level classes in your major. Your program may also have corequisites — courses you have to take in conjunction with other courses during the same semester (a chemistry lab alongside your chemistry class). Some other essential topics:

- How long will it take you to achieve your degree or certificate?

- How many credits must you take to graduate on time? (Note: If you're on financial aid, doing a work-study program, or a college athlete, you may have to take a minimum number of credits per term.)

- What are the salary potential and career opportunities for majors you are considering?

- Are the school and your program accredited? (This is boring but important: If your program isn't accredited, it will make it a lot harder to find a

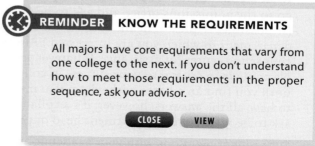

REMINDER KNOW THE REQUIREMENTS

All majors have core requirements that vary from one college to the next. If you don't understand how to meet those requirements in the proper sequence, ask your advisor.

CLOSE   VIEW

job after you graduate. Employers favor applicants who have degrees from accredited institutions.)

- What are the prerequisites for your major?
- Could you include studies for a minor?
- Could you accelerate your studies by going for a combined or interdepartmental degree?
- If you've taken any AP credits or placement exams, could you use them to fulfill some of your requirements?

What to take away. Be sure to leave with a printout of your current course schedule, including notes for the classes you might take in the next term and beyond. At many colleges, you and your advisor will set up a five- to seven-semester plan online.

A final word on selecting your classes. Most full-time students take four to six courses a semester. Most classes don't meet every day. With that in mind, decide which classes you want to take, find out which days and times they meet, and make sure they don't overlap. Your class timetable will impact almost every aspect of your college life, so find ways to make your schedule work for you. A few rules of thumb:

- To get the classes you want, make sure to register as early as possible — in person or online.
- Resist the temptation to cram all your classes into one or two days. It's better to aim for a manageable workload, spread out over the week.
- Go for a mix of more demanding and less demanding classes. (Especially at the beginning, you might not realize how challenging college classes can be or how much outside work they entail.)
- Factor in your biorhythms. Are you a morning person, or do you study better in the afternoon?
- Make time for studying. Embrace the 2-for-1 rule: For every hour you spend in class, you should plan to study two more hours out of class. That's the standard, so keep it in mind when you're planning your schedule.

What if your academic advisor isn't very helpful? It happens. In that case, go to the admissions office and ask to be assigned to a different advisor. (If possible, request a dean, admissions counselor, or instructor in the department in which you are interested.) Alternately, drop by the campus counseling center for assistance. Whatever you do, don't give up. Academic planning is so critical to your success in college that it's worth persevering until you find an advisor with whom you mesh. Don't expect your advisor to have all the answers, however; it's a collaborative effort. When in doubt, ask to be referred to a department head or professor who can help.

Subsequent meetings with your academic advisor. Touch base with your advisor at least once a semester, if not more. It's important to stay connected and make sure you're on a positive track. If both of you have mapped out your five- to seven-semester plan online, keep in touch by email. Some questions to ask along the way:

- Have there been any changes to your curriculum? Programs change requirements occasionally, so it's smart to keep an eye on the horizon.
- If you're thinking of officially withdrawing from a class, are you sure that doing so won't hurt you later?
- Are you still taking classes in the right order?
- If you are at a two-year school and plan to transfer to a four-year school, what courses do you need to take to satisfy the major requirements at the four-year institution?
- If you're considering graduate school, are you meeting the criteria? Will your grades qualify you for your program of interest?

1.3 How to Choose a Major

You could post a list of the twenty hottest jobs on the wall and throw darts at it, but it's not the best idea. When you talk to people who love their jobs, there's one common thread: Something about their respective fields grabbed them from the start. By this point, you should know yourself well enough to identify your interests and find a mentor who can help you make them marketable. Also, keep an open mind: Your major won't necessarily dictate your future career, but it will lead you to new possibilities.

What to do if you're really stuck. The investment is too steep to let yourself drift. So go back to step one: Visit your campus career office and take an aptitude test to find a field tailored to your personality, talents, and interests. While you're there, flip through job directories. Test-drive a few different types of careers via internships, job shadowing, co-op programs, or volunteer work. Above all, connect with your college alumni network to meet people who are already working in fields that appeal to you. It's an excellent way to get advice on potential majors and career paths, not to mention useful contacts and job leads.

Should you explore a double major or minor? It depends on your interests and career goals. If you dream of becoming a museum curator, for example, a double major in English and art history could come in handy. If you want to become a financial analyst and write investment reports, it might make sense to major in economics and minor in English. If you decide on a double major, and if your school allows it, you may need to get approval from both departments and a dean.

Failure to launch. If you've been at college for three or four semesters and can't settle on a major, you may want to meet with a college counselor or psychologist to figure out what the roadblock is. Personal problems or a lack of support at home might be holding you back. Or you may have emotional issues that make you fear success or failure. There's help for that, too.

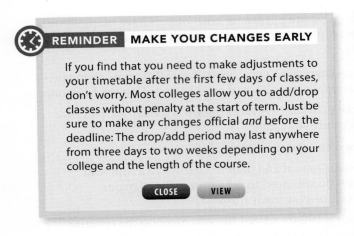

REMINDER MAKE YOUR CHANGES EARLY

If you find that you need to make adjustments to your timetable after the first few days of classes, don't worry. Most colleges allow you to add/drop classes without penalty at the start of term. Just be sure to make any changes official *and* before the deadline: The drop/add period may last anywhere from three days to two weeks depending on your college and the length of the course.

CLOSE   VIEW

How can you find a great mentor, and why is it important? Look behind any success story and you'll invariably find that there was a mentor involved. Anyone can benefit from an experienced person's guidance and support. Your academic advisor might become your mentor. Alternately, you may connect with an alumnus, a graduate student, a family friend, an instructor in your field of interest, or perhaps even your department head. Take advantage of your college alumni center to find helpful contacts. Join a student or academic club, or look for a work-study job in your academic department, so that you can connect with your instructors and learn about internships, jobs, graduate programs, and scholarships.

1.4 Handy Tips for Part-Time Students

Consider taking a prep course. Before you register for classes, you may be asked to take a placement test to determine what level of instruction will best suit your needs. Don't be alarmed if you find yourself in lower-level English composition and upper-level math, or if you're asked to take a developmental prep course. Students arrive at college with different abilities and degrees of preparation, and administrators want to ensure that you don't get in over your head or waste your time. Don't fear the prep course: It might sound like a way to delay graduation, but it will actually boost your chances for success.

How to plan your schedule when you work or have family commitments. Finding balance is everything. Start by figuring out how much school you can handle. Keep in mind that in college, you'll spend more time on your studies *outside* of the classroom than in it; you simply have more responsibility for your education than you did in high school. Find classes that fit around your other commitments. Most universities offer weekend, evening, or online classes. While it can feel like a lot to juggle, your college *wants* to work with you to make sure you are succeeding. Talk to an advisor about how to make it all fit.

Whatever you do, try not to overextend yourself. Make sure that you have a supportive network of helpful family members and friends. And try to be realistic. If you have too much on your plate, you may want to postpone college for a while.

1.5 Mistakes Smart Students Make

Not having a plan. Choosing your courses haphazardly can be an expensive waste of time. In fact, choosing the right major is vital to your success. In a study conducted by the Community College Survey of Student Engagement of the College of Education at the University of Texas at Austin, only a quarter of the students in the survey reported talking about career plans with an instructor or advisor.

Overloading on coursework. If you exceed the maximum courseload, you may need the dean's approval. Even then, it's not ideal. Your grades may suffer, and you might miss out on the full experience of college and all the things that go with it—the friendships, valuable mentor connections, and extracurricular activities. By simply plowing through school, you may rob yourself of something important.

Getting permanently derailed. There are all sorts of reasons you might have to take a leave of absence from college. You may need to take a semester off to earn money for tuition. You might get sick, be pregnant, or have to care for a family member. In the case of an unexpected detour, the biggest challenge is to stay motivated and focused. Having a solid academic plan will make it easier to pick up where you left off. So will maintaining your connections with an advisor, mentor, or former instructors. Colleges know that education is empowerment, and they love to see students who took a hiatus return to finish their degrees.

Not knowing registration deadlines. It's worth repeating: You need to register for classes *before* the first semester starts. The earlier you register, the more likely you are to get the classes you want. Popular courses fill up quickly.

Not having a backup plan at registration. Even early birds occasionally find that the classes they want are already filled. In case that happens, keep a list of alternative classes. It will make the registration process easier and more relaxing. Scheduling conflicts? Ask your advisor for help.

1.6 Insider Tactics: How Top Students Map Their Academic Paths

The Accidental Scholar   *Stephen Scruby*
History major, *University of Florida*

"My roommate always browsed the course catalog for cool classes. He wanted to take Byzantine history but it didn't fit in his schedule, so he suggested it to me. Everything happened from there. Once I realized that I wanted to be a medieval history major, I felt a lot more interested in going to class and started to care about doing well. Up to then, college kind of seemed like something everyone else wanted me to do."

- **Meet with an academic advisor during first-year orientation.** "My advisor had no better idea of my interests than I did at the time, so she signed me up for general courses. She also showed me how to use the online registration system, which proved invaluable. It can be confusing if you don't know what you're doing."

- **Use the add/drop period to try out different options.** "I've never had a finalized course schedule before the start of term—I always tweak it that first week. Unless you've had the professor before, you have no idea what a course will be like until you sit down in the classroom, get a sense of his or her teaching style, and look at the syllabus."

- **Rely on word of mouth.** "It helps to talk to other students about classes and professors they like, particularly if they're in your major. Or go see the instructor during office hours and ask him or her about the course in person."

- **Once you settle on a major, take as many classes in it as you can.** "I filled my schedule with lots of interesting courses in my field. I figured that even if it turned out to be a ton of work, I'd enjoy it and benefit. The bonus was I got to know several professors in the history department, so I felt a lot more comfortable selecting classes going forward."

- **If you're taking an ongoing series of classes — say, in a language — don't take a break.** "It's always better to take those courses back to back if you can. Stopping in the middle makes it a lot harder to retain the information. Plus, when you're learning a new language, you need to keep doing it for several years to make it stick."

The Working Mother   *Marisol Gonzalez*
Finance major, *Florida International University*

"When I decided to go back to school and finish my business degree, I was already working full time and had two young children. So I had to learn how to become an expert in time management—fast."

- **Consider online courses.** "It can be a great option if you need to juggle school with work and family obligations, but you still have to be dedicated and structured with your time. Even though you're not required to be in a classroom setting for two hours, you have to log on and participate in class and your time is recorded; if you're assigned to watch a video, the computer records that you've seen it. Depending on the professor, you may have to engage your classmates in online conversations or submit group projects together on deadline. All of that is accounted for in your final grade."

- **If you're coming back to college after a break, meeting with an academic advisor is especially important.** "It turned out that the requirements of my business program had changed while I was away. Now there's a global learning requirement, so I'll have to fit that into my class schedule in order to earn my degree."

- **Go easy on yourself.** "Since I already have a hectic schedule, I take only as many courses as I can handle. I want to finish up school as quickly as possible, but I don't want to get sick from the stress. Unless I beef up my summer class schedule, I'll finish in two and a half years. And that's okay."

The Pragmatist   *Debbie Sanchez*
Nursing student, *University of Miami*

"In my nursing program, all of the classes are required and planned out — there's only one elective. I have all the same people in all of my classes because we all follow the same core program."

- **If you're getting a nursing degree, your schedule might be largely predetermined.** "My first semester, my classes were picked for me. The dean's office emailed me my class schedule, but let me schedule my own clinicals: That's when you work in a hospital and practice what you're learning in the classroom and the lab. If I was taking Nursing 307, for example, I had to take Clinical 307. You don't get any credit for a clinical, but you can't pass the class without it."

- **Look for amazing teachers.** "The first semester, I went with whatever clinicals were available and fit in my schedule. The next semester, I asked around and had some idea of who the best clinical instructors were. Then I went out of my way to request them."

- **Don't gauge the difficulty of a class by the credits involved.** "My elective was only a two-credit class and didn't include any clinicals, but I ended up putting in just as much effort as I did in my seven-credit classes. It's nursing — nothing's easy. You have to think."

Time Management

You might be the kind of student who thinks it's normal to spend hours making flash cards and outlining your notes in different colored ink. Or maybe you're an adrenaline junkie, accustomed to starting a twenty-page term paper the night before it's due.

The problem is that both of these approaches carry risk. Goof off and you may fail all your courses. Do nothing but stare at your laptop for weeks on end and you'll wind up dull, sick, and miserable. If you're like most of us, you'll learn more, get better grades, and have more fun in college if you operate somewhere in the middle.

By now, you've probably heard the Latin expression *carpe diem*, which translates to "seize the day" (as in, make time work for you). Mastering the art of time management is one key to your future success and happiness, but learning to actually make time work for you can be problematic. What can you do to take control of your own time? Read on to find out.

2.1 The Case for Time Management

Why bother? We know. Some students don't want to "waste" time on planning and managing their schedules. Instead, they prefer to go with the flow. Unfortunately, the demands of college (not to mention most careers) require serious, intentional strategies. Unless you can afford to hire a personal assistant, your previous "slacker habits" won't carry you through.

To psych yourself up, think of time management as part of your life skill set. If you're trying to remember all the things you need to get done, it's hard to focus on actually doing the work. Organizing your time well accomplishes three things. First, it optimizes your chances for good results so you're not flying by the seat of your pants. Second, it enhances your life by saving you from stress and regret. And finally, it reflects what you value: It's all about doing your best.

Remember that people who learn good time management techniques in college generally soar in their careers. Think about it: If you're more efficient at your job, you'll be able to accomplish more. That will lend you a competitive advantage over your coworkers. Your bosses will learn to depend on you. They'll reward you with interesting projects, promotions, and educational and training opportunities. You'll feel empowered and will fill your workplace with positive vibes. You'll have time for a sizzling social life outside the office. You may even make more money and have less stress than your coworkers.

2.2 Getting in Gear: Taking Charge of Your Time

Freedom can be a dangerous thing. One of the biggest differences between high school and college is that you find yourself with far more independence — and greater responsibility — than you've ever known. If you are continuing your education after a break, you may also be contending with spouse/boss/child obligations, too, and if you're working with distanced learning, you may not be required to make the trip to a campus. But it would be a gigantic mistake to assume that Oprah, rocket scientists, and other type-A folks have some kind of monopoly on organization and focus. You, the ordinary student, can also embrace your inner executive assistant — the one who keeps you on time, on task, and ready for a slice of the action. So how do you begin?

Set some goals. Goals help you figure out where to devote the majority of your time. To achieve your goals, you need to do more than just think about them. You need to act. This requires setting some short-term and long-term goals. When determining your long-term goals, it is important to be honest and realistic with yourself. Goals should be challenging, but they should also be attainable. Be sure they align with your abilities, values, and interests. Do you want to go on to further schooling? Have you decided what career you want to pursue? Mulling over these questions can help you start thinking about where you want to be in the next five to ten years. Dreaming up long-term goals can be exciting and fun; however, reaching your goals requires undertaking a number of steps in the short term.

Try to be very specific when determining your short-term goals. For example, if you're committed to becoming an expert in a certain field, you'll want to commit yourself to every class and internship that can help you on your way. A specific goal would be to review your school's course catalog, identify the courses you want to take, and determine when you must take them. An even more specific goal would be to research interesting internship opportunities in your field of study. The good news about goals is that each small step adds up.

Identify one long-term goal and identify three steps you can take to achieve your goal.

Long-Term Goal _____

Steps toward your goal

1. _____

2. _____

3. _____

Know your priorities. To achieve your goals, set your life priorities so that you're steadily working toward them.

- **Start out with a winner's mentality:** Make sure your studies take precedence. Having worked so hard to get to college, you cannot allow other activities and *The Office* reruns to derail your schoolwork. Review your current commitments and prepare to sacrifice a few — for now. Whatever you do, talk to your family, your boss, and your friends about your college workload and goals so that everyone's on the same page. When you have a looming deadline, be firm. Emphasize that no amount of badgering will succeed in getting you to go to the '90s theme party during finals week.

- **Next, start preparing for your future:** Visit your campus career center and schedule an assessment test to home in on your talents and interests. Or, if you know what career you want to pursue, talk with a professional in that field, your guidance counselor, a professor, or an upper-class student in your chosen major to find out what steps you need to take to get the results you want, starting now. What skills and experiences should be on your résumé when you graduate that will make you stand out from the pack? Make a plan, prioritize your goals, and then make a time-management schedule.

- **Balance is key:** Being realistic about your future and goals may mean making big sacrifices. Be realistic about the present, too. Always include time in your schedule for people who are important to you and time on your own to recharge.

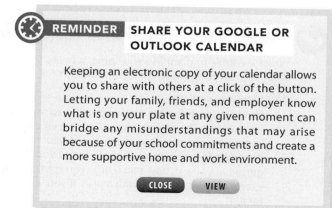

REMINDER **SHARE YOUR GOOGLE OR OUTLOOK CALENDAR**

Keeping an electronic copy of your calendar allows you to share with others at a click of the button. Letting your family, friends, and employer know what is on your plate at any given moment can bridge any misunderstandings that may arise because of your school commitments and create a more supportive home and work environment.

CLOSE   VIEW

Embrace the 2-for-1 rule. For every hour you spend in class at college, you should plan to study two hours more outside of class (even — or especially — if you're doing remote learning and "in" and "out" of class happens in the same place). That's the standard, so keep it in mind when you're planning your schedule. The bottom line is that you simply carry more responsibility for your education in college than you did in high school.

Own your class schedule. Your schedule will impact almost every aspect of your college life. Before you register, think about how to make your schedule work for you.

- **Start with your biorhythms.** Do you study more effectively in the day or the evening or a combination of both? Ideally, you should devote your peak hours — when you're most alert and engaged — to schoolwork. Schedule other activities, like laundry, email, exercise, and socializing, for times when it's harder to concentrate.

- **If you live on campus,** you might want to create a schedule that situates you near a dining hall at mealtimes or lets you spend breaks between classes at the library. Feel free to slot breaks for relaxation and catching up with friends. But beware the midday nap: You risk feeling lethargic afterward or, even worse, oversleeping and missing the rest of your classes. If you attend a large college or university, be sure to allow adequate time to get from one class to another.

- **If you're learning remotely,** try to create an environment where you're able to focus and concentrate on the lesson at hand. Attending virtual classes might seem convenient, and it can be, but if you don't give a class period your full attention, you may wind up playing catch-up later.

- **Try to alternate classes with free periods.** Also, seek out instructors who'll let you attend lectures at alternative times in case you're absent. If they offer flexibility with due dates for assignments, all the better.

CONTROL FACTOR: KNOW WHAT YOU *CAN* AND *CAN'T* CONTROL

When it comes to planning your time, it helps to know the difference between what you can control and what you can't control.

What you can control

- **Making good choices.** How often do you say, "I don't have time"? Probably a lot. But truth be told, you have a choice when it comes to most of the major commitments in your life. You also control many of the small decisions that keep you focused on your goals: when you wake up, how much sleep you get, what you eat, how much time you spend studying, and whether you get exercise. So be a person with a plan. If you want something, you'll make time for it.

- **Doing your part to succeed.** Translation: Go to all your classes; arrive on time; buy all the required textbooks; keep track of your activities; complete every reading and writing assignment on time; take notes in class; and, whenever possible, participate and ask questions.

- **Managing your stress levels.** Organization is the key to tranquility and positive thinking. Manage your time well, and you won't be tormented with thoughts of all the things that need doing. Psychologists have found that free-floating anxiety can turn even your subconscious thoughts into a horror show. Want to avoid unnecessary stress? Plan ahead.

What you can't control

- **Knowing how much you'll need to study right off the bat.** Depending on the kind of high school you went to (and the types of courses you took there), or if it has been a while since you've had to study, you might be more or less prepared than your college classmates. If your studying or writing skills lag behind, expect to put in a little extra time until you're up to speed.

- **Running into scheduling conflicts.** If you find it hard to get the classes you need, you can seek help from a dean, an academic advisor, or someone in the college counseling center.

- **Needing a job to help pay your way.** Just follow the experts' rule of thumb: If you're taking a full course load, do your best to avoid working more than fifteen hours a week. Any more than that and your academic work could suffer.

- If you're a commuter student or carry a heavy workload, you might be tempted to schedule your classes in blocks without breaks. But before you do this, consider the following:
  - The fatigue factor
  - No last-minute study periods before tests
  - The possibility of having several exams on the same day
  - In case of illness, falling behind in all classes

2.3 Four Time-Wasting Habits to Avoid

1. Procrastinating   Maybe you're a perfectionist — in which case, avoiding a task might be easier than having to live up to your own very high expectations (or those of your parents or instructors). Maybe you object to the sheer dullness of an assignment, or you think you can learn the material just as well without doing the work. Maybe you even fear success and know just how to subvert it.

None of these qualifies as a valid reason to put off your work. They're just excuses that will get you in trouble. Fortunately, doing tasks you don't like is excellent practice for real life.

Alert: Procrastination is a slippery slope. Research shows that procrastinators are more likely to develop unhealthy habits like higher alcohol consumption, smoking, insomnia, poor diet, and lack of exercise. Make sure you get these tendencies under control early. Otherwise, you could feel overwhelmed in other aspects of your life, too.

Tricks to Stop Procrastination:

1. *Break big jobs down into smaller chunks.* Spend only a few minutes planning your strategy and then act on it.

2. *Reward yourself* for finishing the task by watching your favorite TV show or playing a game with your kids or friends.

3. *Find a quiet, comfortable place to work* that doesn't allow for distractions and interruptions. Don't listen to music or keep the TV on. If you study in your room, shut the door.

4. *Treat your study time like a serious commitment.* That means no phone calls, email, text messages, or social media. You can rejoin society later.

5. *Consider the consequences if you don't get down to work.* You don't want to let bad habits derail your ability to achieve good results *and* have a life.

2. Overextending yourself   Feeling overextended is a huge source of stress for college students. Why? Well, what constitutes a realistic workload varies significantly from one person to another. Being involved in campus life is fun and important, and it's crucial not to let your academic work take a back seat.

- **Learn to say no — even if it means letting other people down.** Don't be tempted to compromise your priorities.

- **But don't give up all nonacademic pursuits.** On the contrary, students who work or participate in extracurricular activities often achieve higher grades than their less-active counterparts partly because of the important role that time management plays in their lives.

- **If you're truly overloaded with commitments and can't see a way out . . .** You may need to drop a course before the drop deadline. It may seem drastic, but a low grade on your permanent record is even worse. Become familiar with your school's add/drop policy to avoid penalties. If you receive financial aid, keep in mind that in most cases you must be registered for a minimum number of credit hours to be considered a full-time student and maintain your current level of aid. Be sure before you drop!

3. Losing your focus   Too many first-year college students lose sight of their goals. Translation: They spend their first term blowing off classes and assignments, then either get placed on probation or have to spend years clawing their way back to a decent GPA. So plan your strategy and keep yourself focused and motivated for the long haul.

4. Running late

Punctuality is a virtue. Rolling in late to class or review sessions shows a lack of respect for both your instructors and your classmates. Arrive early and avoid using your phone in class, texting, doing homework for

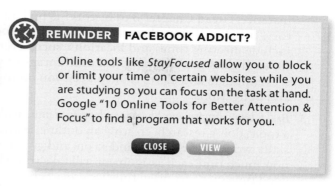

REMINDER   **FACEBOOK ADDICT?**

Online tools like *StayFocused* allow you to block or limit your time on certain websites while you are studying so you can focus on the task at hand. Google "10 Online Tools for Better Attention & Focus" to find a program that works for you.

CLOSE   VIEW

another class, falling asleep, talking, whispering, or leaving an online class for a moment to switch over your laundry. Part of managing your time is freeing yourself to focus on the present and on other people who inhabit the present with you. Note: Respecting others is a habit that can work wonders in your career and personal life.

2.4 Two Indispensable Tools to Keep You on Track

Once you enter college or the working world, you must immediately do the following: Write down everything you need to do; prioritize your tasks; and leave yourself constant reminders. The good news is that a little up-front planning will make your life infinitely easier and more relaxing. For one thing, you'll be less likely to screw up. On top of that, you'll free your brain from having to remember all the things you need to get done so you can focus on actually doing the work. Two key items will help you plan to succeed.

A planner or calendar Find out if your college sells a special planner in the campus bookstore with important dates and deadlines already marked. Or, if you prefer to use an online calendar or the one that comes on your computer or smartphone, that's fine, too. As you schedule your time, follow a few basic guidelines:

1. *Pick a time frame that works best for you.* If you want a big-picture sense of how your schedule plays out, try setting up a calendar for the whole term or for the month. For a more detailed breakdown of what you need to accomplish in the near future, a calendar for the week or even the day may be a better fit. Of course, there's no need to limit yourself—use more than one type of calendar if that works for you. If you're keeping your calendar on a smartphone, you can toggle among different views—day, week, and month.

2. *Enter all of your commitments.* Once you've selected your preferred time frame, it's time to record your commitments and other important deadlines. These might include your classes, assignment due dates, work hours, family commitments, and so on. Be specific. For

instance, "Read Chapter 8 in history" is preferable to "Study history," which is better than simply "Study." To be even more specific, include meeting times and locations, social events, and study time for each class you're taking. Take advantage of your smartphone and set reminders and alerts to help keep you on top of all your activities and obligations.

3. *Break large assignments like research projects into smaller bits,* such as choosing a topic, doing research, creating an outline, learning necessary computer skills, writing a first draft, and so on, and give them deadlines. Estimate how much time each assignment will take you. Then get a jump on it. A good time manager often finishes projects before the actual due dates to allow for emergencies.

4. *Watch out for your toughest weeks during the term.* If you find that paper deadlines and test dates fall during the same week or even the same day, you can alleviate some of the stress by finding time to finish some assignments early to free up study and writing time. If there's a major conflict, talk it over with your professor and find a way to work around it. Professors will be more likely to help you if you talk with them early instead of last minute.

5. *Update your planner/calendar constantly.* Enter all due dates as soon as you know them. Be obsessive about this.

6. *Check your planner/calendar every day* (at the same time of day if that helps you remember). You'll want to review the current week and the next week, too.

7. *When in doubt, turn to a type-A classmate for advice.* A hyperorganized friend can be your biggest ally when it comes to making a game plan.

A to-do list The easiest way to remember all the things you need to do is to jot them down in a running to-do list — updating as needed. You can do this on paper or use an online calendar or smartphone to record the day's obligations. There are also a number of great free apps available to help you stay organized. Try one or two to see if it might be a good fit.

1. **Prioritize.** Rank items on your list in order of importance. Alternately, circle or highlight urgent tasks. Exclamation points and stars — it's all good.

2. **Every time you complete a task, cross it off the list.** (This can be extremely satisfying.)

3. **Move undone items to the top of your next list.** (Less satisfying, but smart and efficient.)

4. **Start a new to-do list every day or once a week.** It shouldn't be just about academics. Slot in errands you need to run, appointments, email messages you need to send, and anything else you need to do that day or week.

EASY WAYS TO MAXIMIZE YOUR TIME

- **Carry work with you.** If you have a lull between classes, use it to review material from the previous class and prepare for the next one. Take advantage of waiting time (on the bus or between appointments) to study. You'll be more likely to remember what you've learned in class if you review or copy your notes as soon as you reasonably can.

- **Discipline yourself with routines.** You might want to get up early to prepare, or set fixed study hours after dinner or on weekend afternoons.

- **Don't multitask.** Even though you might be quite good at it, or think you are, the reality is — and research shows — that you'll be able to do your most effective studying and retain the most information if you concentrate on one task at a time.

- **Study with friends.** You can help each other grasp tricky concepts and memorize important facts and dates.

- **Be flexible.** Disruptions to your plans don't come with ample warning time. Build extra time into your schedule so that unanticipated interruptions don't prevent you from meeting your goals.

2.5 Insider Tactics: How Top Students Manage Their Time

The Early Bird   *Martha Flot*
Education major in Florida

"I learned a long time ago that if I don't start my work early, it's not going to happen. I always open my books right after the kids are off to school, and begin with the easiest assignments. I feel really productive and get into the swing of things before tackling the harder stuff. It's kind of like the warm-up before practice."

- **Digitally bolster your memory.** "I keep everything in my smartphone calendar — for me, that's the best way to stay organized. I set reminders for all of my study groups and upcoming assignments. If it's a big exam, I'll set the reminder a week in advance to give myself plenty of time to prepare."

- **Exercise.** "I always try to exercise before I sit down for an exam or a long study session, too. Studies show that exercise boosts your blood circulation, so you can think better and feel more awake. For me, it makes a huge difference."

- **Beware of overcommitting.** "I used to be a huge people pleaser. Trying to please everyone and juggling my role as a mother, wife, and student, I learned fast that I couldn't do that and still get all my work done. Once I started prioritizing, my friends and family have been responsive and supportive. It helps having a husband who manages his time well; you grow and learn from it."

The Night Owl   *John Dietz*
Architecture major in Florida

"My first two years of college forced me to be a morning person. But as an upperclassman, I have the freedom to pick classes that start in the afternoon, so I've reverted to being nocturnal: I usually study or work in my design studio until 2 or 3 A.M."

- **Go digital.** "I take my computer to all my classes, so I keep a detailed calendar there. My work schedule changes frequently, so I always type that in along with all my assignments."

- **Beware of perfectionism.** "As an architect, you could spend your whole life designing something. Often I really have to tell myself to stop and go on to the next thing."

- **Find a part-time job that offers flexible hours and lets you study.** "I work at the gym on campus, where each shift is just three hours long. They only hire students, so they're very accommodating if I need to change my schedule. Plus, mostly I get to sit at the check-in desk and review my notes."

The Juggler   *Carolina Buckler*
Business and political science major in Indiana

"Having a double major means a heavier workload, but it's doable in my subjects. My roommate — who's studying engineering and puts in a lot more hours than I do — couldn't have handled a heavier workload because of his major."

- **Start things sooner rather than later.** "That especially helps with group projects because it's hard to find time in everyone's schedule to get together. If you meet early, you can divide up the work."

- **Make sure your employer knows your academic commitments.** "I work twelve to fifteen hours a week as a teacher's assistant in the political science department. The professors will automatically understand if I need to take a study day. Around finals, they give everyone a week off."

- **Socialize at mealtimes.** "My friends and I meet for dinner at 5 P.M. It sounds ridiculously early, but I've found that it makes me less likely to waste time: Instead of trying to start something for an hour or so before dinner, I get back around 6:30 and jump right into homework."

For more help managing your time, see pages 89–91 for advice on taking effective notes and tips for taking tests.

PART TWO

Breaking Down the Patterns

3

Reading Essays

Reading is essential in all your college courses. To get the most out of your reading, you should approach the **texts** you read — books, articles, websites, and so on — in a practical way, always asking yourself what information they can offer you. You should also approach assigned readings critically, just as you approach your own writing when you revise.

Reading critically does not mean challenging or arguing with every idea; rather, it means considering, commenting, questioning, and assessing. Most of all, it means being an active rather than a passive reader. Being an **active reader** means participating in the reading process: approaching a reading assignment with a clear understanding of your purpose, previewing a text, highlighting and annotating it, and perhaps outlining it — all *before* you begin to respond in writing to what you have read.

To gain an understanding of your **purpose** — your reason for reading — you should start by answering some questions.

QUESTIONS ABOUT YOUR PURPOSE

- Will you be expected to discuss what you are reading? If so, will you discuss it in class? In a conference with your instructor?

- Will you have to write about what you are reading? If so, will you be expected to write an informal response (for example, a journal entry) or a more formal one (for example, an essay)?

- Will you be tested on the material?

3.1 Previewing

When you **preview** a text, you don't read it word for word; instead, you **skim** the text to get a sense of the writer's main idea, key supporting points, and general emphasis. You should begin by focusing on the title, the first paragraph (which often contains a purpose statement or overview), and the last paragraph (which often contains a summary of the writer's points). You should also look at each paragraph's first sentence. As you skim, you should look for clues to the passage's content and the writer's emphasis in other **visual signals**, such as headings, boxed words, and images.

GUIDELINES FOR PREVIEWING

- Look at the title.
- Look at the author's name.
- Look at the opening paragraph, searching for the sentence that best expresses the main idea.
- Look at the closing paragraph, searching for a summary of the writer's ideas.
- Look at each paragraph's first sentence.
- Look at headings and subheadings.
- Look at *italicized* and **boldfaced** words.
- Look at numbered lists.
- Look at bulleted lists (like this one).
- Look at graphs, charts, tables, diagrams, photographs, and other images.
- Look at any information that is boxed.
- Look at any information that is in color.

When you have finished previewing, you should have a general sense of what the writer wants to communicate.

Practice

Select a reading that has been assigned to you from *Patterns for College Writing*. Preview the reading in preparation for class discussion. As you read, try to identify the writer's main idea and key supporting points. Write this information down in a notebook or Word document and bring it with you so that you are prepared for the class discussion.

3.2 Highlighting

After you have previewed a passage, read it again, this time more carefully. As you read, keep a pen or pencil (or a highlighter pen) handy so that you can **highlight**, using underlining and symbols to identify important information. This active reading strategy will reinforce your understanding of the writer's main idea and key supporting points and will help you to see the relationships among them. (If you want to highlight material from a book that you do not own, photocopy the passage first.)

USING HIGHLIGHTING SYMBOLS

- <u>Underline</u> or highlight key ideas.
- Box or circle words or phrases you want to remember.
- Place a check mark (✓) or star (✳) next to an important idea.
- Place a double check mark (✓✓) or double star (✳✳) next to an especially significant idea.
- Draw lines or arrows to connect related ideas.
- Put a question mark beside a word or idea that you do not understand.
- Number the writer's key supporting points or examples.

Highlight freely, but try not to highlight too much. Remember, you will eventually have to read every highlighted word, phrase, and sentence — and your study time is limited. Highlight only the most important, most useful information — for example, definitions, examples, and summaries.

 REMINDER   KNOWING WHAT TO HIGHLIGHT

You want to highlight what's important — but how do you *know* what's important?

- Look for the same **visual signals** that you looked for when you did your previewing. Many of the ideas you will need to highlight will probably be found in material that is visually set off from the rest of the text — opening and closing paragraphs, lists, and so on.
- Look for **verbal signals** — words and phrases like *however, therefore, another reason,* and *the most important point* — that often introduce key points. (Some of these verbal signals are included in the list that follows.)

Together, these visual and verbal signals will give you clues to the writer's meaning and emphasis.

CLOSE   VIEW

RECOGNIZING USING VERBAL SIGNALS

- Look for phrases that signal emphasis ("The *primary* reason"; "The *most important* idea").
- Look for repeated words and phrases.
- Look for words that signal addition (*also, in addition, furthermore*).

- Look for words that signal time sequence (*first, after, then, next, finally*).
- Look for words that identify causes and effects (*because, as a result, for this reason*).
- Look for words that introduce examples (*for example, for instance*).
- Look for words that signal comparison (*likewise, similarly*).
- Look for words that signal contrast (*unlike, although, in contrast*).
- Look for words that signal contradiction (*however, on the contrary*).
- Look for words that signal a narrowing of the writer's focus (*in fact, specifically, in other words*).
- Look for words that signal summaries or conclusions (*to sum up, in conclusion*).

Here is how a student highlighted a passage from an introductory American history textbook. The passage focuses on the position of African Americans in society in the years immediately following World War II. Because the passage includes no visual signals apart from the title and paragraph divisions, the student looked carefully for verbal signals to guide her highlighting.

"I spent four years in the army to free a bunch of Frenchmen and Dutchmen," an African-American corporal declared, "and I'm hanged if I'm going to let the Alabama version of the Germans kick ✓ me around when I get home." Black veterans as well as civilians resolved that the return to peace would not be a return to the racial ✓ injustices of prewar America. Their political clout had grown with the migration of two million African Americans to northern and western cities, where they could vote and participate in ongoing struggles to end discrimination in housing and education. Pursuing civil rights through the courts and Congress, the National Association for the Advancement of Colored People (NAACP) counted half a million members.

In the postwar years, individual African Americans broke through the color barrier, achieving several "firsts." Jackie Robinson integrated major league baseball, playing for the Brooklyn Dodgers and braving abuse from fans and players to win the Rookie of the Year Award in 1947. In 1950, Ralph J. Bunche received the Nobel Peace Prize for his United Nations work, and Gwendolyn Brooks was awarded the Pulitzer Prize for poetry. Charlie "Bird" Parker, Ella Fitzgerald, and a host of other Black musicians were hugely popular across racial lines.

**   Still, for most African Americans little had changed, especially in the South, where violence greeted their attempts to assert their (1) rights. Armed white men turned back Medgar Evers (who would become a key civil rights leader in the 1960s) and four other veterans (2) trying to vote in Mississippi. A mob lynched Isaac Nixon for voting in Georgia, and an all-white jury acquitted the men accused of his (3) murder. In the South, political leaders and local vigilantes routinely intimidated potential Black voters with threats of violence and warnings that they could lose their livelihoods.

—James L. Roark et al., *The American Promise*, Fifth Edition

The student who highlighted this passage was preparing for a meeting of her study group. Because the class would be taking a midterm the following week, she needed to understand the material.

The student began her highlighting by placing check marks beside two important advances for African Americans cited in paragraph 1 and by drawing arrows to specific examples of Blacks' political influence. (Although she thought she knew the meaning of the word *clout*, she circled it anyway and placed a question mark above it to remind herself to check its meaning in a dictionary.)

In paragraph 2, she boxed the names of prominent postwar African Americans and underlined their contributions, circling and starring the key word "firsts." She then underlined and double-starred the entire passage's main idea — the first sentence of paragraph 3 — numbering the examples in the paragraph that support this idea.

Practice

Review the highlighted passage from the history textbook that begins on the previous page. How would your own highlighting of this passage be similar to or different from the sample student highlighting?

Practice

Reread the selection your instructor assigned for the practice activity on page 26. As you read, highlight the passage by underlining and starring main ideas, boxing and circling keywords, and indicating important points with check marks. Circle each unfamiliar word and put a question mark above it.

3.3 Annotating

As you highlight, you should also annotate what you are reading. **Annotating** a passage means reading critically and making notes — of questions, reactions, reminders, and ideas for discussion or writing — in the margins or between the lines. Keeping a record of ideas as they occur to you will help prepare you to discuss the reading with your classmates — and, eventually, to write about it.

Considering the following questions as you read will help you to read critically and to write useful annotations.

QUESTIONS FOR READING CRITICALLY

- What is the writer saying? What do you think the writer is suggesting or implying? What makes you think so?
- What is the writer's purpose (his or her reason for writing)?
- What kind of audience is the writer addressing?
- What is the writer's main idea?
- Is the writer responding to another writer's ideas?
- How does the writer support his or her points? Does the writer use facts? Opinions? Both?
- What kind of supporting details and examples does the writer use?
- Does the writer include enough supporting details and examples?
- Does the writer seem well informed? Reasonable? Fair?
- Do you understand the writer's vocabulary?
- Do you understand the writer's ideas?
- Do you agree with the points the writer is making?
- How are the ideas presented like (or unlike) those presented in other texts you have read?

 REMINDER **MAKING USEFUL ANNOTATIONS**

As you annotate, be careful not to write too much or too little; good annotations fit in the margins or between the lines or on a small sticky note on the page. You should *not* write your annotations on a separate sheet of paper. If you do, you will be tempted to write too much, and you can easily lose track of where a particular note belongs or what point it comments on. (And if you lose the sheet of paper, you will lose all of your notes and thoughts.) Think of your annotations as a study aid that you can consult when you return to the text a few days later. If you have made useful annotations, they will help you follow the writer's ideas and remember what is most important in the text.

CLOSE   VIEW

The following passage reproduces the student's highlighting of the American history textbook from pages 28–29 and also illustrates her annotations.

Achievements of
African Americans:

Military

Politics

"I spent four years in the army to free a bunch of Frenchmen and Dutchmen," an African-American corporal declared, "and I'm hanged if I'm going to let the Alabama version of the Germans kick ✓ me around when I get home." Black veterans as well as civilians resolved that the return to peace would not be a return to the racial ✓ injustices of prewar America. Their political clout had grown with the migration of two million African Americans to northern and western cities, where they could vote and participate in ongoing struggles to end discrimination in housing and education. Pursuing civil rights through the courts and Congress, the National Association for the Advancement of Colored People (NAACP) counted half a million members.

(?)   = power

Sports

World politics

Literature

Music

In the postwar years, individual African Americans broke through the color barrier, achieving several *"firsts."* Jackie Robinson integrated major league baseball, playing for the Brooklyn Dodgers and braving abuse from fans and players to win the Rookie of the Year Award in 1947. In 1950, Ralph J. Bunche received the Nobel Peace Prize for his United Nations work, and Gwendolyn Brooks was awarded the Pulitzer Prize for poetry. Charlie "Bird" Parker, Ella Fitzgerald, and a host of other Black musicians were hugely popular across racial lines.

In South, voters
intimidated

** Still, for most African Americans little had changed, especially in the South, where violence greeted their attempts to assert their ① rights. Armed white men turned back Medgar Evers (who would become a key civil rights leader in the 1960s) and four other veterans ② trying to vote in Mississippi. A mob lynched Isaac Nixon for voting in Georgia, and an all-white jury acquitted the men accused of his ③ murder. In the South, political leaders and local vigilantes routinely intimidated potential Black voters with threats of violence and warnings that they could lose their livelihoods.

— James L. Roark et al., *The American Promise,* Fifth Edition

In her annotations, this student put some of the writer's key ideas into her own words and recorded ideas she hoped to discuss in her study group.

Practice

Reread the selection from *Patterns for College Writing.* As you reread, refer to the Questions for Reading Critically (page 30), and use them to guide you as you write your own ideas and questions in the margins. Note where you agree or disagree with the writer, and briefly explain why. Quickly summarize any points you think are particularly important. Take time to look up any unfamiliar words you have circled, and write brief definitions for them.

3.4 Outlining

Another technique you can use to understand a reading assignment better is **outlining**. Unlike a **formal outline**, which follows fairly strict conventions—for example, major heads are identified by roman numerals, less important heads by capital letters, and so on—an **informal outline** is easy to construct. An informal outline can also be a valuable reading tool: It shows you which ideas are more important than others, and it shows you how ideas are related.

REMINDER   **CONSTRUCTING AN INFORMAL OUTLINE**

To construct an informal outline of a reading assignment, follow these guidelines.

1. Write or type the passage's main idea at the top of a sheet of paper.

2. At the left margin, write down the most important idea of the first paragraph or section of the passage.

3. Indent the next line a few spaces, and list the examples or details that support this idea.

4. As ideas become more specific, indent further. (Ideas that have the same degree of importance are indented the same distance from the left margin.)

5. Repeat this process with each paragraph or section of the passage.

Note: Your word-processing program's outline function will automatically format the different levels of your outline.

CLOSE   **VIEW**

The student who highlighted and annotated the textbook passage on pages 28–29 made the following informal outline to help her understand its content.

<u>Main idea</u>: Although African Americans had achieved a lot by the end of World War II, they still faced prejudice and violence.

African Americans as a group had made significant advances.
    Many had served in the military.
    Political influence was growing.
        More African Americans could vote.
        NAACP membership increased.

Individual African Americans had made significant advances.
  Sports: Jackie Robinson
  World politics: Ralph Bunche
  Literature: Gwendolyn Brooks
  Music: Charlie Parker and Ella Fitzgerald

Despite these advances, much remained the same for African Americans, especially in the South.
  Black people faced violence and even lynching if they tried to vote.
  Elected officials and vigilantes threatened potential voters.

Practice

Working on your own or in a small group, make an informal outline of your assigned reading from *Patterns*. Refer to your highlighting and annotations as you construct the outline. When you have finished, check to make sure your outline shows which ideas the writer is emphasizing and how those ideas are related.

3.5 Summarizing

Once you have previewed, highlighted, annotated, and outlined a text, you may want to *summarize* it to help you understand it better. A **summary** retells, *in your own words*, what a text is about. A summary condenses, so it leaves out all but the main idea and perhaps the key supporting points. A summary omits supporting examples and details, and it does *not* include your own ideas or opinions.

To summarize a text, follow these guidelines.

1. Review your outline.

2. Consulting your outline, restate the main idea *in your own words*.

3. Consulting your outline, restate the key supporting points. Add linking words and phrases between sentences where necessary.

4. Reread the original text to make sure you have not left out anything significant.

REMINDER   AVOIDING PLAGIARISM IN SUMMARIES

To avoid accidentally using the exact language of the original, do not look at the original while you are writing your summary. If you want to use a distinctive word or phrase from the original, put it in quotation marks.

CLOSE   **VIEW**

The student who highlighted, annotated, and outlined the passage from the history textbook wrote the following summary.

> Although African Americans had achieved a lot by the end of World War II, they still faced prejudice and even violence. As a group, they had made significant advances, which included military service and increased participation in politics, as indicated by voting and NAACP membership. Individual African Americans had also made significant advances in sports, world politics, literature, and music. Despite these advances, however, much remained the same for African Americans after World War II. Their situation was especially bad in the South. For example, African Americans still faced the threat of violence and even lynching if they tried to vote. Elected officials and vigilantes also discouraged Black people from voting, often threatening them with economic retaliation or even violence.

Practice

Write a brief summary of your assigned reading in *Patterns*. Use your informal outline as a guide, and remember to keep your summary short and to the point. (Note that your summary will be shorter than the original passage.)

3.6 Reading in College, in the Community, and in the Workplace

In college, in your life as a citizen of a community, and in the workplace, you will read material in a variety of different formats — for example, textbooks, newspapers, websites, and job-related memos, emails, blog posts, and reports.

Although the active reading process you have just reviewed can be applied to all kinds of material, various kinds of reading often require slightly different strategies during the previewing stage. One reason for this is that different kinds of reading may have different purposes — to present information, to persuade, and so on. Another reason is that the various texts you read are aimed at different audiences, and different audiences require different signals about content and emphasis. For these reasons, you need to look for different kinds of verbal and visual signals when you read different kinds of material.

Reading Textbooks

Much of the reading you do in college is in textbooks (like this one). The purpose of a textbook is to present information, and when you read a textbook, your goal is to understand that information. To do this, you need to figure out which ideas are most important as well as which points support those key ideas and which examples illustrate them.

CHECKLIST: READING TEXTBOOKS

Look for the following features as you preview.

- **Boldfaced** and *italicized* words, which can indicate terms to be defined
- Boxed checklists or summaries, which may appear at the ends of sections or chapters
- Bulleted or numbered lists, which may list key reasons or examples or summarize important material
- Diagrams, charts, tables, graphs, photographs, and other visuals that illustrate the writer's points
- Marginal quotations and definitions
- Marginal cross-references
- Web links

Reading News Articles

As a student, employee, and citizen, you read school, community, local, and national newspapers in print and online. Like textbooks, newspapers communicate information. In addition to containing relatively straightforward news articles, newspapers also contain editorials (which aim to persuade) as well as feature articles (which often entertain as well as inform).

CHECKLIST: READING NEWS ARTICLES

Look for the following features as you preview.

- Headlines
- Boldfaced headings within articles
- Labels like *editorial, commentary,* or *opinion,* which indicate that an article is the writer's opinion
- Brief biographical information at the end of an opinion piece
- Phrases or sentences set in **boldface** (to emphasize key points)
- The article's first sentence, which often answers the questions *who, what, why, where, when,* and *how*
- The **dateline**, which tells you the city the writer is reporting from
- Photographs, charts, graphs, and other visuals
- In *print news articles,* related articles that appear on the same page — for example, boxed information or **sidebars**, which are short articles that provide additional background on people and places mentioned in the article
- In *online news articles,* links to related articles, reader comments, or other useful material

Reading Online

In schools, businesses, and community settings, people go online for information. However, because many websites are busy and crowded, reading them can require you to work hard to distinguish important information from not-so-important material.

CHECKLIST: READING WEB PAGES

Look for the following features as you preview.

- The site's URL designation (.com, .org, .gov, and so on)
- Links to other sites (often underlined in blue)
- Graphics
- Color
- Headings
- Boxed material
- Placement of images and text on the page
- Type size
- Photographs

Reading on the Job

In your workplace, you may be called on to read memos, letters, emails, and reports. These documents are often addressed to a group rather than to a single person. (Note that the most important information is often presented *first*—in a subject line or in the first paragraph.)

CHECKLIST: READING ON THE JOB

Look for the following features as you preview.

- Numbered or bulleted lists of tasks or problems (numbers indicate the order of the items' importance)
- The first and last paragraphs and the first sentence of each body paragraph, which often contain key information
- **Boldfaced**, <u>underlined</u>, or *italicized* words
- In a report, visuals that illustrate key concepts
- In electronic communications, the person(s) addressed, the subject line, and links to the web
- In a memo or a report, headings that highlight key topics or points

REVIEW CHECKLIST: READING FOR ACADEMIC SUCCESS

- Become an active reader. (See page 25.)
- Preview your reading assignment. (See page 25.)
- Highlight your reading assignment. (See page 26.)
- Annotate your reading assignment. (See page 29.)
- Outline your reading assignment. (See page 32.)
- Summarize your reading assignment. (See page 33.)
- Learn how to read different kinds of texts. (See page 34.)

Writing Essays

Your words matter. Using them effectively is not only important in school but also in life. How clearly you can express your ideas to others — in school, on the job, and in your community — will determine how well you perform in college, how far you advance in your career, and how effective you are as a community leader.

- In college, you are frequently required to write as part of your coursework to complete essay assignments, to write research papers, to respond to assigned readings, and to answer exam questions. For example:
- For job applications, you will need to create a resume and write cover letters.
- At work, you might write a memo, a letter, a proposal, or a report.
- As a member of your community, you might write a letter or email to a government agency or to the editor of your local newspaper.
- In your personal life, you might respond to emails, post on social networking sites and blogs, and text friends.

Clearly, writing is an inherent part of life, but what about essays? How does writing essays prepare you for success in school and beyond? Writing essays fosters good writing by developing your ability to think critically, argue persuasively, and analyze effectively. Mastery of these skills will lead to higher achievement in all your college classes and in the real world.

4.1 Moving through the Writing Process

Writing is never a single act but a process. When you write an essay — a group of paragraphs focused on a single subject — you begin by planning what you will write about and then move on to organizing your ideas. Next, you spend time drafting and revising. The final steps involve proofreading and editing. Collectively, these steps are known as the **writing process**.

Although these steps may appear to be linear, you will find yourself moving forward and backward through the writing process. That's because the writing process is also **recursive**, which means it loops back around. In this chapter, you will learn effective strategies for moving through the writing process to produce well-thought-out essays.

4.2 Understanding Essay Structure

The essays you write in college will follow a similar pattern that consists of an introduction, several body paragraphs, and a conclusion. This format is a good starting point for students because it provides a useful framework for their ideas.

- The essay's first paragraph, the **introduction**, begins with opening remarks that create interest and closes with a **thesis statement** that presents the essay's main idea.

- The **body** of the essay consists of several **body paragraphs**, and each paragraph contains one point that supports the thesis statement. That point appears as the **topic sentence** of the paragraph. The other sentences in the paragraph support the topic sentence with **evidence** in the form of descriptive details, examples, explanations, facts, or reasons.

- **Transitional words and phrases** lead readers from sentence to sentence and from paragraph to paragraph.

- The last paragraph, the **conclusion**, ends the essay. The conclusion often includes a **summary statement** that reinforces the thesis.

REMINDER **TEST YOUR ESSAY**

The first letters of these four key elements — **T**hesis statement, **E**vidence, **S**ummary statement, and **T**ransitions — spell **T E S T**. As you begin the revision process, you can **T E S T** the essays you write to see whether they include all the elements of an effective essay.

CLOSE   VIEW

ESSAY

INTRODUCTION

Opening remarks introduce the subject being discussed in the essay. The **thesis statement** presents the essay's main idea or the claim being made about the essay's subject.

> **FIRST BODY PARAGRAPH**
>
> The **topic sentence** states the essay's first point.
> **Evidence** supports the topic sentence.
> **Transitional words and phrases** connect the supporting details and show how they are related.

> **SECOND BODY PARAGRAPH**
>
> The **topic sentence** states the essay's second point.
> **Evidence** supports the topic sentence.
> **Transitional words and phrases** connect the supporting details and show how they are related.

> **THIRD BODY PARAGRAPH**
>
> The **topic sentence** states the essay's third point.
> **Evidence** supports the topic sentence.
> **Transitional words and phrases** connect the supporting details and show how they are related.

> **CONCLUSION**
>
> The **summary statement** reinforces the thesis, summarizing the essay's main idea and the points used to support the thesis.
> **Concluding remarks** present the writer's final thoughts on the subject.

The following essay by Jennifer Chu illustrates the structure of an essay. (Note that transitional words and phrases are <u>underlined</u>.)

Becoming Chinese American

Introduction

Although I was born in Hong Kong, I have spent most of my life in the United States. However, my parents have always made sure that I did not forget my roots. They always tell stories of what it was like to live in Hong Kong. To make sure my brothers and sisters and I know what is happening in China, my parents subscribe to Chinese cable TV. When we were growing up, we would watch the celebration of the Chinese New Year, the news from Asia, and Chinese movies and music videos. <u>As a result, even though I am an American, I value many parts of traditional Chinese culture.</u>

Thesis statement

Topic sentence (states essay's first point)

The Chinese language is an important part of my life as a Chinese American. Unlike some of my Chinese friends, I do not think the Chinese language is unimportant or embarrassing. <u>First,</u> I feel

First body paragraph

Evidence (supports topic sentence)

that it is my duty as a Chinese American to learn Chinese so that I can pass it on to my children. In addition, knowing Chinese enables me to communicate with my relatives. Because my parents and grandparents do not speak English well, Chinese is our main form of communication. Finally, Chinese helps me identify with my culture. When I speak Chinese, I feel connected to a culture that is over five thousand years old. Without the Chinese language, I would not be who I am.

Topic sentence (states essay's second point)

Second body paragraph

Evidence (supports topic sentence)

Chinese food is another important part of my life as a Chinese American. One reason for this is that everything we Chinese people eat has a history and a meaning. At a birthday meal, for example, we serve long noodles and buns in the shape of peaches. This is because we believe that long noodles represent long life and that peaches are served in heaven. Another reason is that to Chinese people, food is a way of reinforcing ties between family and friends. For instance, during a traditional Chinese wedding ceremony, the bride and the groom eat nine of everything. This is because the number nine stands for the Chinese words "together forever." By taking part in this ritual, the bride and groom start their marriage by making Chinese customs a part of their life together.

Topic sentence (states essay's third point)

Third body paragraph

Evidence (supports topic sentence)

Religion is the most important part of my life as a Chinese American. At various times during the year, Chinese religious festivals bring together the people I care about the most. During Chinese New Year, my whole family goes to the temple, where we say prayers and welcome others with traditional New Year's greetings. After leaving the temple, we all go to Chinatown and eat dim sum until the lion dance starts. As the colorful lion dances its way down the street, people beat drums and throw firecrackers to drive off any evil spirits that may be around. Later that night, parents give children gifts of money in red envelopes that symbolize joy and happiness in the coming year.

Summary statement (reinforces essay's thesis)

Conclusion

My family has taught me how important it is to hold on to my Chinese culture. When I was six, my parents sent me to a Chinese-American grade school. My teachers thrilled me with stories of Fa Mulan, the Shang Dynasty, and the Moon God. I will never forget how happy I was when I realized how special it is to be Chinese. This is how I want my own children to feel. I want them to be proud of who they are and to pass their language, history, and culture on to the next generation.

Although Jennifer Chu's essay contains all the necessary components of a well-written essay, you can be certain it did not start out that way. In the following sections, you will learn about the steps in the writing process that take you from nebulous idea to completed essay.

4.3 Starting Your First Draft

If writing essays makes you anxious, you are not alone. Staring at a blank page waiting for a flash of brilliance makes all writers uncomfortable. Even the most successful and highly regarded writers experience those same feelings when they sit down to write. Critically acclaimed author Judith Ortiz Cofer — whose essay, "The Myth of the Latin Woman," appears in your textbook — admitted that even after having dozens of her poems, essays, and short stories published, her confidence as a writer lasted right until the moment she "faced the next blank page" (Cofer 228).

Whether you are a student or a professional writer, getting started is the most challenging step in the writing process. That is why it is so important not to procrastinate. Giving yourself plenty of time to explore your subject and experiment with topics will greatly reduce the stress associated with beginning an essay. For additional help, you should review Chapter 2 in *Patterns for College Writing*. This chapter provides you with guidance on getting started using strategies such as freewriting, brainstorming, and clustering. These strategies will help you move from a general subject to the topic of your essay and then develop its main idea or thesis. Once you complete these first steps, you can select the points you will discuss in support of that thesis and arrange them in the order in which you plan to write about them. As you develop your ideas and begin writing, keep the following recommendations in mind:

1. **Move through the writing process one step at a time.** Students who utilize the writing process — planning, organizing, drafting, revising, proofreading, and editing — score higher on their essays and experience less stress than students who do not.

2. **As you draft your essay, make certain it has a thesis-and-support structure.** Writing an essay is like a taking a journey, and the thesis statement keeps you focused on your destination. The supporting details act as a map and show you how to arrive at your destination.

3. **Create a working title, a temporary title that reflects your main idea.** You can revise it later so that it accurately describes the content of your completed essay, but a working title helps you stay focused on your thesis.

4. **Do not write and revise at the same time.** In other words, do not strive to perfect each sentence before you commit it to paper. Revising is a form of critiquing, and when you are working on your first draft, your focus should be on creating. Attempting to do both at the same time is strenuous and ineffective.

Practice

Exercise 1: Brainstorming

The COVID-19 pandemic shifted a lot of professional and educational experiences wholly online. Working in groups, use brainstorming to generate five possible topics that relate to this subject and its significance to college students today. Then develop a thesis statement based on one of those topics.

Exercise 2: Freewriting

Students tend to be self-conscious as they write, constructing sentences as if an invisible critic were scrutinizing every word they type, looking for errors and demanding perfection. For this exercise, you will place imaginary duct tape on the mouth of your invisible critic. Then, you will write for five minutes without stopping. Do not worry about whether your sentences make sense or contain grammar errors. Just keep writing. You may write about whatever is on your mind, or you may choose (1) one of the writing prompts below.

1. Describe your current surroundings, where you are at this exact moment. Include sights, sounds, smells, and physical sensations (for example, a hard chair or a cold room). Finally, include your feelings about those sensory experiences.

2. Write about food: your favorite foods, your favorite restaurants, foods you hate, foods that reflect your culture. If you had to eat one food for the rest of your life, what would it be? When do you eat? Why do you eat? How often do you eat?

3. Write ten sentences that begin with "I remember." Write down whatever comes to mind, whether it is from your childhood or last night. Don't examine the ideas that come to mind. Don't try to recall details. Just complete a sentence and then move on to the next one.

4. Imagine that you have just won the lottery and are now one of the few billionaires in the world. What will you buy with all that money? What will you do differently? What will stay the same? Write down every idea that comes to mind without pausing to assess its practicality.

Freewriting on a regular basis — in a journal, for instance — will build your writing muscles and diminish the power of a blank page to frighten you.

4.4 Revising Your First Draft

Starting your essay may be the most challenging step in the writing process, but revising your essay is the most important one. Revision is an integral part of all good writing. Do not be discouraged if you are unhappy with your writing during the initial stages. Most good writing begins that way. It is the time and effort you invest in the revision process — not the quality of your first efforts — that will determine the quality of the final product. The revision process allows you to take a rough draft that may be disorganized or shallow and transform it so that it contains all the components of a well-written essay. The most skilled writers spend a great deal of time swapping out words, changing sentence structure, reorganizing paragraphs, and adding details that are rich in depth and texture. Revision may sound like a lot of hard work, but it is at the heart of all good writing. It would be a mistake to believe that if writing does not come easily to you, you are not good at it. Writing is hard work for everyone.

Practice

Exercise 1: Backward Outline

During the revision process, you can check the effectiveness of your essay by creating a backward outline. Use this method to assess the effectiveness of the following paragraph by identifying its main idea or topic sentence, each reason provided in support of that idea and the details used to develop each reason. Do the reasons support the main idea? Is the evidence convincing? What is your opinion about the order in which the reasons appear? Finally, is there anything missing in this paragraph? Does it contain a closing statement? Are there transitional words to connect each reason? After you complete the form below, revise this paragraph so that it includes any missing components.

Study-in-Place

Thanks to COVID-19, I have had to go from face-to-face classes to attending classes online, and it has been a challenge for me. I struggle to complete assignments at home where there are so many distractions and interruptions. Last week when I was trying to read *Beowulf* (not the easiest poem to read) my neighbor had a buzz saw going all day, and I couldn't concentrate. I prefer the order of a classroom where the professor is up front and controls who speaks and when. During one of our online meetings, someone mentioned *Tiger King*, the Netflix documentary that everyone's been watching during the pandemic. Suddenly, everyone was trying to talk at the same time. I really miss my fellow students. In the library or in the classroom, it was comforting to see other students all working toward the same goal, and I enjoyed being able to complain to a fellow classmate, "That exam was intense!"

Topic Sentence: _____

Reason 1: _____

Details that develop that reason: _____

_____

Reason 2: _____

Details that develop that reason: _____

_____

Reason 3: _____

Details that develop that reason: _____

_____

Closing statement: _____

STUDENT WRITER: A First Draft

Following is the first draft of first-year composition student Jared White's essay.

Going Back to School

I was out of school for six years after I graduated from high school. The decision to return to school was one I had a lot of difficulty making. I had been around enough to know that without more education, I would really struggle, but I always found reasons for not taking the plunge. However, after a lot of thinking, I realized that my reasons for not going to college were just excuses. Although I realized it would be difficult in some ways, I decided that if I really wanted to attend college full time, I could.

My first excuse for not going to college was that I couldn't afford to go to school full time. I had worked since I finished high school, but I hadn't put much money away. I kept wondering how I would pay for books and tuition. I needed to support myself and pay for rent, food, and car expenses. I was working as a house painter, and a house I was painting belonged to a college instructor. Painting wasn't hard work, but it was boring. I'd start in the morning and work without a break until lunch. We began talking. When I told him about my situation, he told me I should look at our local community college. He also told me about some loans and grants I'd probably be able to apply for. I went online and looked at the college's website. I found out that tuition was one hundred dollars a credit, less than I thought it would be. If I got just one of the grants he mentioned, I might be able to make it.

Now that I had taken care of my first excuse, I had to deal with my second — that I hadn't been a good student in high school.

When I was a teenager, I didn't care much about school. School bored me to death. Probably as a result, I got bad grades. Now that I was considering going back to school, though, I wondered what price I would have to pay for my earlier immaturity. The answer to this question was not as bad as I thought it would be. According to the community college's website, all I needed to be admitted was a high school diploma and county residence. I would have to take some placement tests, but I would be judged on my ability, not my high school grades. I knew I could do better if I made a real effort to study harder and smarter. The website was easy to navigate, and I had no problem finding information.

I had a hard time picturing myself in college. My friends were just like me; they all went to work right after high school. I had no role model or mentor who could give me advice. I thought I was just too old for college. After all, I was probably at least six years older than most of the students. How would I be able to keep up with the younger students in the class? I hadn't opened a textbook for years, and I'd never really learned how to study. Most of my fears disappeared during my first few weeks of classes. I saw a lot of students who were as old as I was, and some were even older. Studying didn't seem to be a problem, either. I actually enjoyed learning. History, which had put me to sleep in high school, suddenly became interesting. So did math and English. It soon became clear to me that I was going to like being in college.

Going to college as a full-time student has changed my life, both personally and financially. I am no longer the same person I was in high school. I allowed disinterest and insecurity to hold me back. Now, I have options that I didn't have before. When I graduate from community college, I plan to transfer to the state university and get a four-year degree.

Practice

Reread Jared's first draft. What changes would you suggest? What might he have added? What might he have deleted? Which of his supporting details and examples do you find most effective?

4.5 TESTing Your Essay

When you have finished your draft, the first thing you should do is "test" what you have written to make sure it includes all the elements of an effective essay.

Thesis Statement
Evidence
Summary Statement
Transitions

If your essay includes these four **T E S T** elements, you are off to a very good start. If it does not, you will need to add whatever is missing.

T E S T ing for a Thesis

The first thing you do when you **T E S T** your essay is to make sure it has a clear **thesis statement (T)** that identifies the essay's main idea. By stating the main idea, your thesis statement helps to unify your essay.

When Jared **T E S T** ed the draft of his essay, he decided that his thesis statement clearly stated his main idea. (His marginal note appears below.)

Jared's Introduction

Thesis clearly states what I want to say about going to college.

I was out of school for six years after I graduated from high school. The decision to return to school was one I had a lot of difficulty making. I had been around enough to know that without more education, I would really struggle, but I always found reasons for not taking the plunge. However, after a lot of thinking, I realized that my reasons for not going to college were just excuses. <u>Although I realized it would be difficult in some ways, I decided that if I really wanted to attend college full time, I could.</u>

T E S T ing for Evidence

The next thing you do when you your **T E S T** essay is to check your **evidence (E)** to make sure that the body of your essay includes enough supporting details to support your thesis. Remember that without evidence, your essay is simply a series of unsupported general statements. A well-developed essay includes enough evidence to explain, illustrate, and clarify the points you are making.

When Jared **T E S T** ed his draft for evidence, he decided that he should add more examples and details in his body paragraphs and delete some irrelevant ones. (His marginal notes appear below.)

Jared's Body Paragraphs

Are details about painting necessary?

<u>My first excuse for not going to college was that I couldn't afford to go to school full time.</u> I had worked since I finished high school, but I hadn't put much money away. I kept wondering how I would pay for books and tuition. I needed to support myself and pay for rent, food, and car expenses. I was working as a house painter, and a house I was painting belonged to a college instructor. Painting

Add more about how I thought I could cover the tuition.

wasn't hard work, but it was boring. I'd start in the morning and work without a break until lunch. We began talking. When I told him about my situation, he told me I should look at our local community college. He also told me about some loans and grants I'd probably be able to apply for. I went online and looked at the college's website. I found out that tuition was one hundred dollars a credit, less than I thought it would be. If I got just one of the grants he mentioned, I might be able to make it.

T E S T ing for a Summary Statement

The third thing you do when you **T E S T** your essay is to look at your con-clusion to make sure it includes a **summary statement (S)**. Most often, your conclusion will begin with this statement, which reinforces your essay's thesis. By reinforcing your thesis, this summary statement helps to **unify** your essay.

When Jared **T E S T** ed his draft for a summary statement, he thought that his summary statement adequately reinforced the main idea of his essay. (His marginal note appears below.)

Jared's Conclusion

Conclusion is too short, but summary statement is OK.

Going to college as a full-time student has changed my life, both personally and financially. I am no longer the same person I was in high school. I allowed disinterest and insecurity to hold me back. Now, I have options that I didn't have before. When I graduate from community college, I plan to transfer to the state university and get a four-year degree.

T E S T ing for Transitions

The last thing you do when you **T E S T** your essay is to make sure that it includes **transitions (T)**, words and phrases that connect your ideas. Make sure you have included all the transitions you need to tell readers how one sentence (or paragraph) is connected to another. Including transitions makes your essay **coherent**, with its sentences arranged in a clear, logical sequence that helps readers understand your ideas.

By linking sentences and paragraphs, transitions emphasize the relation-ship between ideas and help readers follow your essay's logic. By reminding readers of what has come before, transitions prepare readers for new informa-tion and help them understand how it fits into the discussion. In this sense, transitions are the glue that holds the ideas in your essay together.

Transitions are categorized according to their function. For example, they may indicate **time order** (*first, second, now, next, finally,* and so on), **spatial order** (*above, behind, near, next to, over,* and so on), or **logical order** (*also, although, therefore, in fact,* and so on). For a full list of transitions, see page 58 in *Patterns for College Writing.*

When Jared **T E S T** ed his draft for transitions, he realized that although he had included some transitional words and phrases (shaded), he needed to add more of them to connect his ideas. (His marginal notes appear below.)

Jared's Thesis + Body Paragraphs

Although I realized it would be difficult in some ways, I decided that if I really wanted to attend college full time, I could.

My first excuse for not going to college was that I couldn't afford to go to school full time. I had worked since I finished high school, but I hadn't put much money away. I kept wondering how I would pay for books and tuition. I needed to support myself and pay for rent, food, and car expenses. I was working as a house painter, and a house I was painting belonged to a college instructor. Painting wasn't hard work, but it was boring. I'd start in the morning and work without a break until lunch. We began talking. When I told him about my situation, he told me I should look at our local community college. He also told me about some loans and grants I'd probably be able to apply for. I went online and looked at the college's website. I found out that tuition was one hundred dollars a credit, less than I thought it would be. If I got just one of the grants he mentioned, I might be able to make it.

Need to show relationship between ideas in this paragraph.

Now that I had taken care of my first excuse, I had to deal with my second — that I hadn't been a good student in high school. When I was a teenager, I didn't care much about school. School bored me to death. Probably as a result, I got bad grades. Now that I was considering going back to school, though, I wondered what price I would have to pay for my earlier immaturity. The answer to this question was not as bad as I thought it would be. According to the community college's website, all I needed to be admitted was a high school diploma and county residence. I would have to take some placement tests, but I would be judged on my ability, not my high school grades. I knew I could do better if I made a real effort to study harder and smarter. The website was easy to navigate, and I had no problem finding information.

Add better transition between these two paragraphs.

I had a hard time picturing myself in college. No one in my family had ever gone to college. My friends were just like me; they all went to work right after high school. I had no role model or mentor who could give me advice. I thought I was just too old for college. After all, I was probably at least six years older than most of the students. How would I be able to keep up with the younger students in the class? I hadn't opened a textbook in years, and I'd never really learned how to study. Most of my fears disappeared during my first few weeks of classes. I saw a lot of students who were as old as I was,

Add transition here.

and some were even older. Studying didn't seem to be a problem, either. I actually enjoyed learning. History, which had put me to sleep in high school, suddenly became interesting. So did math and English. It soon became clear to me that I was going to like being in college.

The final version of Jared's essay appears below. (Marginal annotations have been added to highlight key features of his essay.) Note that the final draft includes all the elements Jared looked for when he **T E S T** ed his essay.

Jared White
Professor Wilkinson
English 120
7 October 2023

Starting Over

Introduction

The other day, my sociology instructor mentioned that half the students enrolled in college programs across the country are twenty-five or older. His remark caught my attention because I am one of those students. I was out of school for six years after I graduated from high school. The decision to return to school was one I had a lot of difficulty making. I had been around enough to know that without more education, I would really struggle, but I always found reasons for not taking the plunge. However, after a lot of thinking, I realized that my reasons for not going to college were just excuses. <u>Although I realized it would be difficult in some ways, I decided that if I really wanted to attend college full time, I could.</u>

Topic sentence (first point)

Examples and details

Body paragraphs

<u>My first excuse for not going to college was that I could not afford to go to school full time.</u> I had worked since I finished high school, but I had not put much money away. I kept wondering how I would pay for books and tuition. I also needed to support myself and pay for rent, food, and car expenses. The solution to my problem came unexpectedly. I was working as a house painter, and a house I was painting belonged to a college instructor. During a lunch break, we began talking. When I told him about my situation, he told me I should look at our local community college. He also told me about some loans and grants I would probably be able to apply for. Later, I went online and looked at the college's website. I found out that tuition was one hundred dollars a credit, less than I thought it would be. If I got just one of the grants he mentioned, I might be able to make it. The money I had saved, along with what I could make painting houses on the weekends, could get me through.

Topic sentence (second point)

Now that I had taken care of my first excuse, I had to deal with my second — that I had not been a good student in high school. When I was a teenager, I did not care much about school. In fact, school bored me. In class, I would stare out the window or watch the second hand on the clock move slowly around. I never bothered with homework. School just did not interest me. Probably as a result, I got bad grades. Now that I was considering going back to school, though, I wondered what price I would have to pay for my earlier and immaturity. The answer to this question was not as bad as I thought it would be. According to the community college's website, all I needed to be admitted was a high school diploma and county residence. I would have to take some placement tests, but I would be judged on my ability, not my high school grades. I knew I could do better if I made a real effort to study harder and smarter.

Examples and details

Body paragraphs

Topic sentence (third point)

My biggest problem still bothered me: I had a hard time picturing myself in college. No one in my family had ever gone to college. My friends were just like me; they all went to work right after high school. I had no role model or mentor who could give me advice. Besides, I thought I was just too old for college. After all, I was probably at least six years older than most of the students. How would I be able to keep up with the younger students in the class? I had not opened a textbook in years, and I had never really learned how to study. However, most of my fears disappeared during my first few weeks of classes. I saw a lot of students who were as old as I was, and some were even older. Studying did not seem to be a problem, either. I actually enjoyed learning. For example, history, which had put me to sleep in high school, suddenly became interesting. So did math and English. It soon became clear to me that I was going to like being in college.

Examples and details

Conclusion

Going to college as a full-time student has changed my life, both personally and financially. I am no longer the same person I was in high school. In the past, I allowed disinterest and insecurity to hold me back. Now, I have options that I did not have before. When I graduate from community college, I plan to transfer to the state university and get a four-year degree. The other day, one of my instructors asked me if I had ever considered becoming a teacher. The truth is, I never had, but now I might. I would like to be able to give students like me the tough, realistic advice I wish someone had given me.

Practice

Reread the final draft of Jared White's essay. Working in a group of three or four students, answer these questions.

- Do you think this draft is an improvement over his first draft (shown on pages 46–47)?

- What other changes could Jared have made?

Be prepared to discuss your group's answers with the class.

SELF-ASSESSMENT CHECKLIST: REVISING YOUR ESSAY

- Does your essay have an introduction, a body, and a conclusion?
- Does your introduction include a clearly worded thesis statement that states your essay's main idea?
- Does each body paragraph have a topic sentence?
- Does each topic sentence introduce a point that supports the thesis?
- Does each body paragraph include enough examples and details to support the topic sentence?
- Are the body paragraphs unified, well developed, and coherent?
- Does your conclusion include a concluding statement that restates your thesis or sums up your main idea?

Additional practice

In an English composition class, students were asked to write about an obstacle they had experienced in school and about their attempts to overcome it. One student decided to write about his struggles with procrastination and planned to use an entry from the journal he had been keeping as part of his corequisite English class. Because journaling is a form of freewriting, this journal entry would need a lot of revising before it could be turned in. Go through the steps in the writing process to determine how he might take this journal entry from freewriting to a finished product.

1. What is the subject of the essay?
2. What would the essay's main idea be? In other words, what is the author saying about the subject?
3. What parts should he leave out, what parts should he keep, and what parts should be developed more?

4. If he decides to move forward and turn this journal entry into an essay, what would a good working title for this essay be?

5. How would you arrange the essay? Would you start the essay in the same way the journal begins, with the biology class, or would you introduce the problem first?

6. In what ways do you think keeping a journal might help you become a better writer?

Tuesday, February 4

Biology class, not my favorite, but today was different. Teacher talked about people who procrastinate. Said their brains are different from people who just dive right in. Shocker. Turns out the amygdala, the part that controls people's "flight or fight" response, is bigger in procrastinators. A big amygdala equals increased fear of failure and trouble staying focused. I'm thinking, dude, if that's true, then my amygdala must be the size of Texas. I worry about failing in school more than I ever let on. She also said our brains are flexible and we can change them. I always thought folks were either born smart or they weren't. But she says it isn't like that. We can make ourselves smarter. I can even shrink my amygdala! She listed some things that will help, like doing breathing exercises, breaking up big assignments into smaller chunks, finding a quiet place to work, stuff like that. She says with enough practice, any student can be successful. Course they pay teachers to say stuff like that. Anyways. Can't hurt to try. Maybe get my parents to stop complaining about my unused "potential." Geez. If they only knew. Nobody suffers more than me when it comes to waiting till the last minute to do my school work. The closer a due date gets, the worse I feel. Finally, I reach a point of sheer terror, when I either gotta do the stupid paper or flunk out. So I work through the night just to turn something in. Not fun. Not even close. I'll do anything to avoid doing that again. EVER. But the best part? I don't feel like such a loser anymore. I'm not lazy. I just have an oversized amygdala, whatever the heck that is.

References

Cofer, Judith Ortiz, and Margaret Crumpton. "An Interview with Judith Ortiz Cofer." *Meridians*, vol. 3, no. 2, 2003, p. 94, www.jstor.org/stable/40338576.

Narration

5.1 Understanding Narration

Narration is writing that tells a story. For example, a narrative paragraph could tell how an experience you had as a child changed you, how the life of Martin Luther King Jr. inspired Americans, or how the Battle of Gettysburg became the turning point in the Civil War. A narrative can recount events that actually happened, or it can be fictional. In any case, all the details should support the narrative's main idea.

5.2 Writing a Narration Essay

Regardless of your assignment or the discipline in which you are writing, you will probably find yourself using narration. As is the case with other patterns of essay development, certain key features are needed to make a narration essay work. When you **TEST** a **narrative** essay (see page 40), make sure it includes all these elements:

- **T** • **Thesis Statement** — The introduction of a narrative essay should include a **thesis statement** that communicates the main idea — the point the essay is making.

- **E** • **Evidence** — The body paragraphs should tell the story, one event at a time, with each event providing **evidence** — examples and details — to support the thesis. Events are usually presented in chronological (time) order. Effective narratives include only those events that tell the story and avoid irrelevant information that could distract or confuse readers.

- **S** • **Summary Statement** — The conclusion of a narrative essay should include a **summary statement** that reinforces the essay's main idea.

- **T** • **Transitions** — Throughout a narrative essay, **transitional words and phrases** should connect events in time, showing how one event leads to the next.

5.3 Organizing a Narrative Essay

When you write a narrative essay, you can discuss one event or several in each paragraph of your essay.

ESSAY MAP: *One Event per Paragraph*

Introduction (includes thesis statement)

First event

Second event — **Evidence**

Third event

Conclusion (includes summary statement)

ESSAY MAP: *Several Events per Paragraph*

Introduction (includes thesis statement)

First group of events

Second group of events — **Evidence**

Third group of events

Conclusion (includes summary statement)

SOME TRANSITIONAL WORDS AND PHRASES FOR NARRATION

As you arrange your ideas in a narrative essay, be sure to use clear transitional words and phrases. These signals help readers follow your narrative by indicating the order of the events you discuss.

after	first . . . second . . . third	specific dates
as	immediately	(for example, "In 2020")
as soon as	later	suddenly
before	later on	then
by the time	meanwhile	two hours (days, months,
earlier	next	years) later
eventually	now	until
finally	soon	when

5.4 Case Study: A Student Writes a Narrative Essay

Here is how one student, Tiffany Forte, wrote a narrative essay in response to the assignment, "Write an informal essay about a goal or dream you had when you were a child." She began the writing process by freewriting to help her think of experiences she could write about.

> . . . *Could write about breaking my arm—funny story, painful outcome. Maybe better to focus on something with lots of detail, like winning the Halloween costume contest. Awesome costume, best ever. Could write about moving to city from suburbs . . . how I changed. Not as bad as I expected. Need to tell a story, maybe from college experiences, or maybe better from childhood. Maybe playing baseball—best dream, worst disappointment. . . .*

After looking over her freewriting, Tiffany listed the experiences that she could write about.

> Breaking my arm
> Winning the Halloween costume contest
> Moving to a new city
> Playing baseball

As she reviewed the experiences on her list, she realized that she could easily write about any of them. She decided, however, to focus on her love of baseball, which was especially meaningful to her now as she began college and thought about pursuing newer dreams.

At this point, Tiffany did some brainstorming to help her think of material to include in her essay. Then, she created an informal outline by listing the main events she planned to discuss in the order in which they occurred.

> Playing Baseball
>> Always played with the boys
>> Good at playing
>
> Watching Baseball
>> Watching Dad
>> Phillies Games
>>> The stadium (description)
>>> Mike Schmidt, my favorite player
>
> Losing Baseball
>> Boys laughing at me
>> No good leagues for girls

Following her informal outline, Tiffany wrote a first draft of her essay. Remembering that narratives should include a lot of details, she added everything she could remember, knowing that she could delete any irrelevant material later on. (When she finished her draft, she realized that she probably needed even more details than she had included.) Read Tiffany's draft, and then answer the questions in the peer-editing worksheet on page 60.

Tiffany Forte, First Draft

Leaving Baseball Behind

When I was little, I was the only girl in the neighborhood where I lived, so I always played with the boys.

Almost every day, we would meet by the big oak tree to get a baseball game going. I was always one of the first to be picked for a team. I was very fast, and I could hit the ball far. I loved baseball more than anything, and I wouldn't miss a game for the world.

My dad played baseball too, and every Friday night I would go to the field with my mother to watch him play. It was just like the big leagues. I loved my dad's games, and I never wanted to leave. There was so much going on, and each pitch in the game was more exciting than the last one.

I loved watching the major league games. The Phillies were my favorite team, and I always looked forward to watching them on television. We would go wild, yelling and screaming at all the big plays. When the Phillies would win, I would be so excited I couldn't sleep; when they would lose, I would go to bed angry, just like my dad.

It was when my dad took me to my first Phillies game that I decided I wanted to be a major league baseball player. The excitement began when we pulled into the parking lot of the old Veterans Stadium. There were thousands of cars. As we walked from the car to the stadium, my dad told me to hold on to his hand and not to let go no matter what. There were people everywhere! They were walking around the stadium and standing in long lines for food and souvenirs. It was the most wonderful thing I had ever seen. When we got to our seats, I looked down at the tiny baseball diamond below and felt as if I were on top of the world.

The cheering of the crowd, the singing, and the chants were almost more than I could stand. I was bursting with enthusiasm. Then, in the bottom of the eighth inning, with the score tied and two outs, the Phillies hit the game-winning home run. The crowd went crazy. When Mike Schmidt came out of the dugout to receive his standing ovation, I felt a lump in my throat and butterflies in my stomach. He was everyone's hero that night, and I could only imagine the pride he must have felt. I slept the whole way home and dreamed of what it would be like to be the hero of the game.

The next day, when I met with the boys at the oak tree, I told them that when I grew up, I was going to be a major league baseball player. They all laughed at me and said I could never be a baseball player because I was a girl. I told them that they were all wrong and that I would show them.

In the years to follow, I played girls' softball, and I was very good. I always wanted to play baseball with the boys, but I couldn't. After a few years, I realized that the boys were right: I was never going to be a major league baseball player. I realized that what I had been told when I was younger wasn't the truth. I couldn't be anything I wanted to be. I couldn't play baseball in the major league.

In time, I would get over the loss of my dream. I found new dreams, acceptable for a young woman, and I moved on to other things. Still, every time I watch a baseball game and someone hits a home run, I get those same butterflies in my stomach and think, for just a minute, about what might have been.

PEER-EDITING WORKSHEET: NARRATION

1. What point is the writer making about the essay's subject? Is this point explicitly stated in a thesis statement? If so, where? If not, can you state the essay's thesis in one sentence?

2. List some details that enrich the narrative. Where could more detail be added? What kind of detail? Be specific.

3. Does the writer vary sentence structure and avoid monotonous strings of similar sentences? Should any sentences be combined? If so, which ones? Can you suggest different openings for any sentences?

4. Should any transitions be added to clarify the order in which events occurred? If so, where?

5. Do verb tenses establish a clear chronological order? Identify any verb tenses you believe need to be changed.

6. Does the writer need to correct any run-on sentences? Point out any fused sentences or comma splices.

7. What could the writer *add* to this essay?

8. What could the writer *delete* from this essay?

9. What is the essay's greatest strength? Why?

10. What is the essay's greatest weakness? What steps should the writer take to correct this problem?

5.5 Analyzing a Narrative Essay

When Tiffany finished her revisions, she prepared a final draft. Read her final draft, and then do the practice exercise that follows it.

My Field of Dreams

When I was young, I was told that when I grew up I could be anything I wanted to be, and I always took for granted that this was true. I knew exactly what I was going to be, and I would spend hours dreaming about how wonderful my life would be when I grew up. One day, though, when I did grow up, I realized that things had not turned out the way I had always expected that they would.

When I was little, I never played with baby dolls or Barbies. I was the only girl in the neighborhood where I lived, so I always played with the boys. We would play army or football or (my favorite) baseball.

Almost every summer afternoon, all the boys in my neighborhood and I would meet by the big oak tree to get a baseball game going. Surprisingly, I was always one of the first to be picked for a team.

I was very fast, and (for my size) I could hit the ball far. I loved baseball more than anything, and I wouldn't miss a game for the world.

My dad played baseball too, and every Friday night I would go to the field with my mother to watch him play. It was just like the big leagues, with lots of people, a snack bar, and lights that shone so high and bright you could see them a mile away. I loved my dad's games. When all the other kids would wander off and play, I would sit and cheer on my dad and his team. My attention was focused on the field, and my heart would jump with every pitch.

Even more exciting than my dad's games were the major league games. The Phillies were my favorite team, and I always looked forward to watching them on television. My dad would make popcorn, and we would sit and watch in anticipation of a Phillies victory. We would go wild, yelling and screaming at all the big plays. When the Phillies would win, I would be so excited I couldn't sleep; when they would lose, I would go to bed angry, just like my dad.

It was when my dad took me to my first Phillies game that I decided I wanted to be a major league baseball player. The excitement began when we pulled into the parking lot of the old Veterans Stadium. There were thousands of cars. As we walked from the car to the stadium, my dad told me to hold on to his hand and not to let go no matter what. When we gave the man our tickets and entered the stadium, I understood why. There were mobs of people everywhere. They were walking around the stadium and standing in long lines for the hot dogs, beer, and souvenirs. It was the most wonderful thing I had ever seen. When we got to our seats, I looked down at the tiny baseball diamond below and felt as if I were on top of the world.

The cheering of the crowd, the singing, and the chants were almost more than I could stand. I was bursting with enthusiasm. Then, in the bottom of the eighth inning, with the score tied and two outs, Mike Schmidt came up to bat and hit the game-winning home run. The crowd went crazy. Everyone in the whole stadium was standing, and I found myself yelling and screaming along with everyone else. When Mike Schmidt came out of the dugout to receive his standing ovation, I felt a lump in my throat and butterflies in my stomach. He was everyone's hero that night, and I could only imagine the pride he must have felt. I slept the whole way home and dreamed of what it would be like to be the hero of the game.

The next day, when I met with the boys at the oak tree, I told them that when I grew up, I was going to be a major league baseball player. They all laughed at me and said I could never be a baseball player because I was a girl. I told them that they were all wrong and that I would show them.

In the years to follow, I played girls' softball in a competitive fast-pitch league, and I was very good. I always wanted to play baseball with the boys, but there were no mixed leagues. After a few years, I realized that the boys from the oak tree were right: I was never going to be a major league baseball player. I realized that what I had been told when I was younger wasn't the whole truth. What no one had bothered to tell me was that I could be anything I wanted to be — as long as it was something that was appropriate for a girl to do.

In time, I would get over the loss of my dream. I found new dreams, acceptable for a young woman, and I moved on to other things. Still, every time I watch a baseball game and someone hits a home run, I get those same butterflies in my stomach and think, for just a minute, about what might have been.

Practice: Analyzing a Narrative Essay

1. Underline the thesis statement. Then, restate it in your own words.

2. What specific events and details support Tiffany's thesis? List as many as you can.

3. Do you think paragraph 2 is necessary? How would Tiffany's essay be different without it?

4. Paraphrase Tiffany's conclusion in your own words. Do you think her conclusion effectively reinforces her essay's main idea?

5. **TEST** Tiffany's essay (see page 55). Does she include all of the necessary elements?

6. What, specifically, did Tiffany change between her first and final drafts? Do you think all of her changes improved her essay?

Description

6.1 Understanding Description

When you write a **description**, you use words to paint a picture for your readers. With description, you use language that creates a vivid impression of what you have seen, heard, smelled, tasted, or touched. The more details you include, the better your description will be.

There are two types of description, and it is important to choose the one that best suits your purpose for writing. If you write an essay using *objective description*, you report only what your senses of sight, sound, smell, taste, and touch tell you ("The columns were ten feet tall and made of white marble"). However, if you write a *subjective description*, you choose details and adjectives that convey your attitude or your feelings about what you observe ("The columns were tall and powerful looking, and their marble surface seemed as smooth as ice"). Keep in mind that many descriptive essays combine these two kinds of description.

6.2 Writing a Descriptive Essay

Whether you choose to write an objective description (which is common in history and the sciences) or a subjective description (which is common in composition classes), you will need to **T E S T** your descriptive essay to be sure that it includes all the necessary elements (see page 40).

T • **Thesis Statement** — A descriptive essay should include a **thesis statement** that expresses the essay's main idea.

E • **Evidence** — The body paragraphs should include supporting **evidence**, descriptive details that support the thesis. Details are arranged in spatial order — for example, from far to near or from top to bottom.

S • **Summary Statement** — The conclusion of a descriptive essay should include a **summary statement** that reinforces the essay's thesis.

T • **Transitions** — A descriptive essay should include **transitional words and phrases** that connect details and show how they are related.

6.3 Organizing a Descriptive Essay

When you plan a descriptive essay, you focus on selecting details that help your readers see what you see, feel what you feel, and experience what you experience. Your goal is to create a single *dominant impression*, a central theme or idea to which all the details relate — for example, the liveliness of a street scene or the quiet of a summer night. This dominant impression unifies the description and gives readers an overall sense of what the person, place, object, or scene looks like (and perhaps what it sounds, smells, tastes, or feels like).

You can arrange details in a descriptive essay in many different ways. For example, you can move from least to most important details, from top to bottom (or from bottom to top or side to side), or from far to near (or near to far). Each of your essay's body paragraphs may focus on one key characteristic of the subject you are describing or on several related descriptive details.

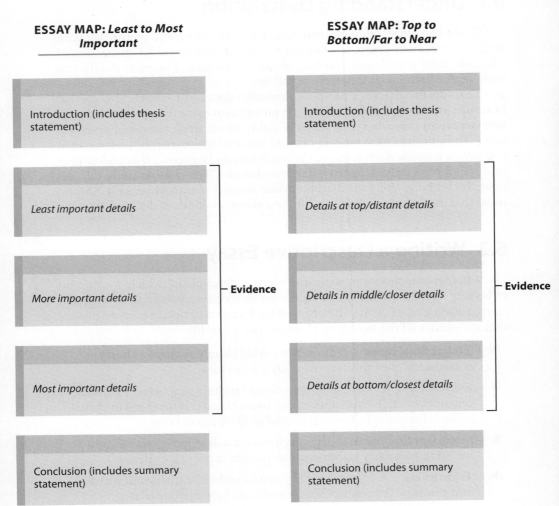

ESSAY MAP: *Least to Most Important*

Introduction (includes thesis statement)

Least important details

More important details — Evidence

Most important details

Conclusion (includes summary statement)

ESSAY MAP: *Top to Bottom/Far to Near*

Introduction (includes thesis statement)

Details at top/distant details

Details in middle/closer details — Evidence

Details at bottom/closest details

Conclusion (includes summary statement)

SOME TRANSITIONAL WORDS AND PHRASES FOR DESCRIPTION

As you arrange your ideas in a descriptive essay, be sure to use appropriate transitional words and phrases to lead readers from one detail to another.

above	in	outside
at the edge	in back of	over
at the entrance	in front of	spreading out
behind	inside	the first . . . the second
below	nearby	the least important . . .
between	next to	the most important
beyond	on	the next
down	on one side . . . on the	under
farther	other side	

6.4 Case Study: A Student Writes a Descriptive Essay

Here is how one student, Mary Lim, wrote a descriptive essay in response to the assignment, "Write an essay about a place that had a profound effect on you." Mary began by making an entry in her writing journal, focusing on places that had made a strong impression.

> Normally, we think of people having a profound effect on us, and don't think that places might do the same thing. However, now that I think about it, there are a number of places that stand out in my mind. College has been a place full of change for me, and it took me a long time to get into the swing of things. My grandmother's house has always been an important location for my entire family because it's where we spend our holidays and where I get to see my cousins, aunts, and uncles. It's in Burma, a country that most of my classmates might not be familiar with. There are many places in Burma that are worth writing about. It's known for strange happenings and exotic scenery. One of the strangest places I ever visited, though, is the Valley of Windmills. The windmills are just outside of Taungaleik and they are very old and scary. Some of them are falling apart, and most of them are covered with dark green moss. There are more than ten thousand of them.

Using her journal entry as a starting point, Mary brainstormed about the Valley of the Windmills and listed all the descriptive details that she could think of.

Burma	Taungaleik
Mysterious	Beautiful
Old	More modern
Full of dense jungles	Active
	Mountainous
	Hard to get to

The Valley	
Between mountains and Taungaleik	Thin air
Beautiful	Stony
Old	Dangerous near the edges of the road
Cool	

The Windmills	
Old	No sails
Haunting	Huge
Gloomy	Weird
Covered in moss	Creepy
Falling apart	Abandoned
Big	

Then, Mary wrote a first draft of her essay. She wanted to get her ideas down on paper while they were fresh. She knew that she could evaluate and polish her draft later, when she revised. Read through Mary's draft, and then answer the questions in the peer-editing worksheet on page 67.

Mary Lim, First Draft

The Valley of Windmills

The windmills stand like dark figures in the misty atmosphere just outside of Taungaleik, a beautiful city in Burma. In this fertile valley there is beautiful and breathtaking scenery, but there are also old, massive, and gloomy structures that can disturb a person deeply. With its jutting, rocky peaks and jungles dense with exotic vegetation that human beings cannot even enter, the Valley of Windmills is a mysterious place that seems to have been ignored by time.

The windmills are immensely old and distinctly evil, some merely turrets. Most of them are covered with dark green moss. Their decayed but still massive forms seem to turn and sneer at visitors. There are still more windmills down the pass, where a circular green plateau lies like an arena below. As far as the eye can see, in every field, above every hut, stand ten thousand iron windmills, silent and sailless. They seem to await only a call from a watchman to clank, whirr, flap, and groan into action. They make you feel cold.

The road to Taungaleik twists out of the coastal flatlands into those heaps of slag, shale, and limestone that are the Tenasserim Mountains in the southern part of Burma. The air grows thinner, and stones become grayer, the highway a little more dangerous at its edges, until, ahead. You have to travel down this road to find the menacing windmills. They straddle the road and stand at intervals up hillsides on either side. Are they boulders? Are they fortifications? Are they broken wooden crosses on graves in an abandoned cemetery? Soon, you can see them for what they really are, but the towering forms are still deeply unsettling to behold.

As you stand at the lip of the valley, contrasts rush in to overwhelm you. Beyond, glittering on the mountainside like a solitary jewel, is Taungaleik. Below, on rolling hillsides, are the dark windmills, still enveloped in morning mist. These ancient windmills can remind a person of the impermanence of life and mystery that still surrounds these hills. In a strange way, the scene in the valley can be disturbing, but it can also offer insight into the contradictions that define life here in Burma.

PEER-EDITING WORKSHEET: DESCRIPTION

1. What is the essay's dominant impression or thesis?

2. What points does the writer emphasize in the introduction? Should any other points be included? If so, which ones?

3. Would you characterize the essay as primarily an objective or subjective description? What leads you to your conclusion?

4. Find some examples of figures of speech. Could the writer have used figures of speech in other places? If so, where?

5. What specific details does the writer use to help readers visualize what is being described? Where could the writer have used more details? Would a visual have helped readers understand what is being described?

6. Are all the details necessary? Can you identify any that seem excessive or redundant? Where could the writer have provided more details to support the thesis or convey the dominant impression?

7. How are the details in the essay arranged? Why are the details arranged in that order? What other arrangement could the writer have used?

8. List some transitional words and phrases the writer uses to help readers follow the discussion. Which sentences need transitional words or phrases to link them to other sentences?

9. Do any sentences contain misplaced or dangling modifiers? If so, which ones?

10. How effective is the essay's conclusion? Does the conclusion reinforce the essay's dominant impression?

6.5 Analyzing a Descriptive Essay

When Mary finished her revisions, she prepared a final draft. Read her final draft, and then do the practice exercise that follows it.

The Valley of Windmills

In my native country of Burma, strange happenings and exotic scenery are not unusual, for Burma is a mysterious land that in some areas seems to have been ignored by time. Mountains stand jutting their rocky peaks into the clouds as they have for thousands of years. Jungles are so dense with exotic vegetation that human beings or large animals cannot even enter. But one of the most fascinating areas in Burma is the Valley of Windmills, nestled between the tall mountains near the beautiful city of Taungaleik. In this fertile valley, there is beautiful and breathtaking scenery, but there are also old, massive, and gloomy structures that can disturb a person deeply.

The road to Taungaleik twists out of the coastal flatlands into those heaps of slag, shale, and limestone that are the Tenasserim Mountains in the southern part of Burma. The air grows rarer and cooler, and stones become grayer, the highway a little more precarious at its edges, until, ahead, standing in ghostly sentinel across the lip of a pass, is a line of squat forms. They straddle the road and stand at intervals up hillsides on either side. Are they boulders? Are they fortifications? Are they broken wooden crosses on graves in an abandoned cemetery?

These dark figures are windmills standing in the misty atmosphere. They are immensely old and distinctly evil, some merely turrets, some with remnants of arms hanging derelict from their snouts, and most of them covered with dark green moss. Their decayed but still massive forms seem to turn and sneer at visitors. Down the pass on the other side is a circular green plateau that lies like an arena below, where there are still more windmills. Massed in the plain behind them, as far as the eye can see, in every field, above every hut, stand ten thousand iron windmills, silent and sailless. They seem to await only a call from a watchman to clank, whirr, flap, and groan into action. Visitors suddenly feel cold. Perhaps it is a sense of loneliness, the cool air, the desolation, or the weirdness of the arcane windmills — but something chills them.

As you stand at the lip of the valley, contrasts rush in to overwhelm you. Beyond, glittering on the mountainside like a solitary jewel, is Taungaleik in the territory once occupied by the Portuguese. Below, on rolling hillsides, are the dark windmills, still enveloped in morning mist. These ancient windmills can remind a person of the impermanence of life and the mystery that still surrounds these hills. In a strange way, the scene in the valley can be disturbing, but it also can offer insight into the contradictions that define life here in Burma.

Practice: Analyzing a Descriptive Essay

1. Paraphrase Mary's thesis statement.

2. What determines the order in which Mary arranges the elements of her description?

3. What details does Mary provide to describe Burma, Taungaleik, and the windmills?

4. Circle the transitions that Mary uses to move readers from one detail to another. What signals do her transitions give readers? Do you think that she included enough transitions? Where could Mary have added more?

5. This essay is primarily a subjective description. Does it include any objective details? If so, where?

6. Summarize the essay's conclusion in your own words.

7. **TEST** Mary's essay (see page 63). Does she include all of the necessary elements?

8. What, specifically, did Mary change between her first and final drafts? Do you think all of Mary's changes improved her essay?

Exemplification

7.1 Understanding Exemplification

Exemplification illustrates a general statement with one or more specific examples. For instance, if you tell some friends that you are having a bad day, you might explain that you got a parking ticket, that you were late for class, and that someone spilled coffee on you in the cafeteria. This support will enable your friends to see that you're having a bad day and give them a clear idea of why.

7.2 Writing an Exemplification Essay

An **exemplification essay** uses specific examples to support a thesis. Personal experiences, class discussions, observations, conversations, and readings can all be good sources of examples. You can use **TEST** to make sure your exemplification essay includes all the necessary elements (see page 40).

- **T** • **Thesis Statement** — The introduction of an exemplification essay should include a clear **thesis statement** that identifies the essay's main idea — the idea the examples will support.

- **E** • **Evidence** — The body paragraphs should present supporting **evidence**, fully developed examples that support the thesis. Each body paragraph should be introduced by a topic sentence that identifies the example or group of related examples that the paragraph will discuss. Examples (and paragraphs) should be arranged in **logical order** — for example, from least to most important or from general to specific. The number of examples you need depends on your thesis. A broad thesis will probably require more examples than a narrow one.

- **S** • **Summary Statement** — The conclusion of an exemplification essay should include a **summary statement** that reinforces the essay's thesis.

- **T** • **Transitions** — An exemplification essay should use appropriate **transitional words and phrases** to connect examples within paragraphs and between one paragraph and another.

7.3 Organizing an Exemplification Essay

In an exemplification essay, each body paragraph can develop a single example or discuss several related examples. The topic sentence should introduce the example (or group of related examples) that the paragraph will discuss. Each example you select should clearly support your thesis.

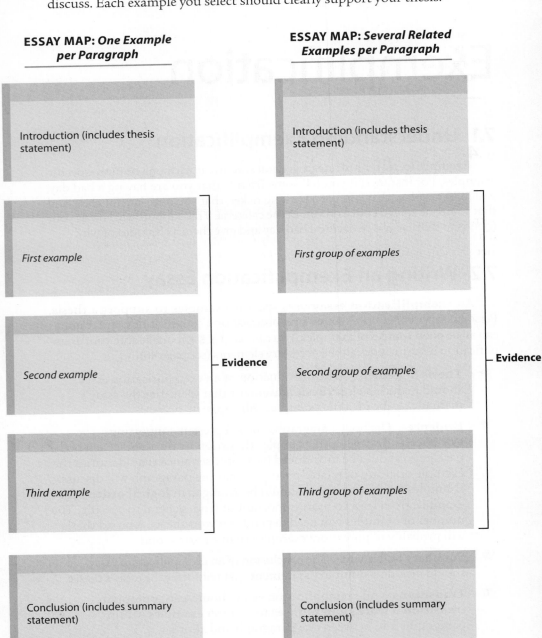

ESSAY MAP: *One Example per Paragraph*

Introduction (includes thesis statement)

First example

Second example ⎤ Evidence

Third example

Conclusion (includes summary statement)

ESSAY MAP: *Several Related Examples per Paragraph*

Introduction (includes thesis statement)

First group of examples

Second group of examples ⎤ Evidence

Third group of examples

Conclusion (includes summary statement)

SOME TRANSITIONAL WORDS AND PHRASES FOR EXEMPLIFICATION

When you write an exemplification essay, be sure to include appropriate transitional words and phrases. These transitions help readers follow your discussion by indicating how your examples are related and how each example supports the topic sentence.

also	furthermore	the most important
finally	in addition	example
first . . . second . . .	moreover	the next example
(and so on)	one example . . .	then
for example	another example	
for instance	specifically	

7.4 Case Study: A Student Writes an Exemplification Essay

Here is how one student, Kristy Bredin, used exemplification to write a letter of application to apply for an internship with *Rolling Stone* magazine. To make sure she included all her qualifications, Kristy brainstormed, listing her professional and academic experience since high school.

> music major
>
> started learning guitar
>
> English major
>
> concessions at AMC Movies
>
> front of house assistant manager at AMC Movies
>
> internship at Taylor and Francis
>
> studied abroad: London
>
> secretary of Lit Society
>
> Lit Society newsletter
>
> passed writing portfolio requirement
>
> president of Lit Society
>
> Editor for *Manuscript*
>
> Editor for *Comeneian*

Then, Kristy reviewed the list, crossing off the items that were not relevant to the internship and that would not help her to make her case.

> music major
>
> ~~started learning guitar~~
>
> English major

~~concessions at AMC Movies~~
~~front of house assistant manager at AMC Movies~~
internship at Taylor and Francis
~~studied abroad: London~~
secretary of Lit Society
Lit Society newsletter
~~passed writing portfolio requirement~~
president of Lit Society
Editor for *Manuscript*
Editor for *Comeneian*

Kristy knew that letters of application had to be short and to the point. She also knew that her organization would be important because she had to present her qualifications as clearly as possible. For this reason, she made an informal outline in which she listed her points along with her supporting examples.

Why I'm interested
  English major
  music major
Why I'm qualified
  Lit Society
  Editor for *Manuscript*
  Editor for *Comeneian*
  internship at Taylor and Francis

Then, Kristy wrote a first draft of her letter of application. She focused on her structure, using the first draft to experiment with how to present her examples in as few words as possible. Read through Kristy's draft and then answer the questions in the peer-editing worksheet on page 76.

Kristy Bredin, First Draft

Dear Ms. Goldstein:

    I am writing to apply for the paid online internship that you posted on RollingStone.com. I believe that both my education and my experience in publishing qualify me for the position you advertised and that I would be a great fit for the *Rolling Stone* team.

I am an English major at Moravian College, with a double major in music and creative writing. While at Moravian College, I have maintained a 3.4 grade point average, of which I am very proud because Moravian is a difficult school. After I graduate in May, I would like to work in the publishing industry because I have always loved the written word. For this reason, I am very interested in your internship. It would give me additional editorial and administrative experience that would help me in my future career. It would also give me insight into how a large-scale publishing operation works and how I might fit into it. An internship at RollingStone.com would also enable me to read, edit, and possibly write articles about popular music — a subject I know a lot about and am very invested in.

I acquired professional editing experience as well as experience posting across platforms this past semester, when I worked as an intern for Taylor and Francis (Routledge) Publishing in New York. I think this experience would be directly relevant to the RollingStone.com position. Throughout college, I have also been involved in writing and editing. I have served as both secretary and president of the Literary Society. I have written, edited, and published its annual newsletter. I have also worked as a tutor in Moravian's Writing Center and as a literature editor for the *Manuscript*, Moravian's literary magazine. Finally, I was a features editor for the *Comeneian*, the student newspaper at Moravian. In these jobs I have gained a good deal of practical experience in publishing as well as insight into dealing with my fellow students.

I believe that my publishing experience and my education make me a good candidate for your paid online internship. As your ad requested, I have enclosed my résumé, information on Moravian's internship program, and several writing samples for your consideration. You can contact me by phone at (484) 625-6731 or by email at stkab@moravian.edu. I look forward to meeting with you to discuss my qualifications.

Sincerely,
Kristy Bredin

PEER-EDITING WORKSHEET: **EXEMPLIFICATION**

1. What strategy does the writer use in the essay's introduction? Would another strategy be more effective?

2. What is the essay's thesis? Does it make a point that the rest of the essay will support with examples?

3. What specific points do the body paragraphs make?

4. Does the writer use one example or several to illustrate each point? Should the writer use more examples? Fewer? Explain.

5. Does the writer use a sufficient range of examples? Are they explained in enough depth?

6. Do the examples add interest? How persuasive are they? List a few other examples that might be more persuasive.

7. What transitional words and phrases does the writer use to introduce examples? What other transitional words and phrases should be added? Where?

8. In what order are the examples presented? Would another order be more effective? Explain.

9. Has the writer used a series of three or more examples in a single sentence? If so, are these examples separated by commas?

10. What strategy does the writer use in the conclusion? What other strategy could be used?

7.5 Analyzing an Exemplification Essay

When Kristy finished her revisions, she prepared a final draft. Read her final draft, and then do the practice exercise that follows it.

1028 Geissinger Street
Bethlehem, PA 18018
September 7, 2023

Kim Goldstein
Rolling Stone
1290 Avenue of the Americas
New York, NY 10104-0298

Dear Ms. Goldstein:

I am writing to apply for the paid online internship that you posted on RollingStone.com. I believe that both my education and my experience in publishing qualify me for the position you advertised.

I am currently a senior at Moravian College, where I am majoring in English (with a concentration in creative writing) and music. Throughout my college career, I have maintained a 3.4 average. After I graduate in May, I would like to find a full-time job in publishing. For this reason, I am very interested in your internship. It would not only give me additional editorial and administrative experience, but it would also give me insight into a large-scale publishing operation. An internship at RollingStone.com would also enable me to read, edit, and possibly write articles about popular music — a subject I know a lot about.

Throughout college, I have been involved in writing and editing. I have served as both secretary and president of the Literary Society and have written, edited, and published its annual newsletter. I have also worked as a tutor in Moravian's Writing Center; as a literature editor for the *Manuscript*, Moravian's literary magazine; and as a features editor for the *Comeneian*, the student newspaper. In these jobs I have gained a good deal of practical experience in publishing as well as insight into dealing with people. In addition, I acquired professional editing experience as well as experience posting across platforms this past semester, when I worked as an intern for Taylor and Francis (Routledge) Publishing in New York.

I believe that my education and my publishing experience make me a good candidate for your position. As your ad requested, I have enclosed my résumé, information on Moravian's internship program, and several writing samples for your consideration. You can contact me by phone at (484) 625-6731 or by email at stkab@moravian.edu. I will be available for an interview anytime after September 23. I look forward to meeting with you to discuss my qualifications.

Sincerely,

Kristy Bredin

Kristy Bredin

Practice: Analyzing an Exemplification Essay

1. What is Kristy's thesis?

2. What reasons for her interest does Kristy give in paragraph 2? What examples of her qualifications does Kristy give in paragraph 3? Which of these paragraphs do you think is more important to her letter?

3. Is Kristy's conclusion effective? What information might be more effective in a different paragraph? Draft a third body paragraph to include before Kristy's conclusion. Then, rewrite her conclusion.

4. What is this letter's greatest strength? What is its greatest weakness?

5. **TEST** Kristy's essay (see page 71). Does she include all of the necessary elements?

6. What, specifically, did Kristy change between her first and final drafts? Do all of Kristy's changes improve her essay? Why or why not?

Process

8.1 Understanding Process

When you describe a process, you tell readers how something works or how to do something. For example, you could explain how the optical scanner at the checkout counter of a food store operates, how to hem a pair of pants, or how to start a blog. A **process** essay tells readers how to complete a process by listing steps in time order—either the order in which they happened or the order in which you need to complete the steps.

There are two types of process essays: *process explanations* and *instructions*. Process explanations walk readers through the steps in a process without any expectation that readers will be performing the process themselves. Instructions are usually much more specific, listing all of the steps necessary to complete the process, and often include lists of materials or supplies, as well as cautions and warnings and possible solutions to common mistakes.

8.2 Writing a Process Essay

Process writing is not as common as some of the other methods, such as narration or description, but it is one of the most practical. You can use **TEST** to make sure your process essay includes all the necessary elements (see page 40).

- **T** • **Thesis Statement**—A process essay should include a **thesis statement** that expresses the essay's main idea, identifying the process you will discuss and telling why it is important or why you are explaining it.

- **E** • **Evidence**—The body paragraphs should provide supporting **evidence**—examples and details—that explains all the steps in the process and supports the essay's thesis. Each paragraph's topic sentence should identify the step (or group of related steps) that the paragraph will explain. Steps should be presented in strict chronological (time) order.

S • **Summary Statement** — The conclusion of a process essay should include a **summary statement** that reinforces the essay's thesis.

T • **Transitions** — A process essay should include **transitional words and phrases** that link the steps in the process and show how they are related.

8.3 Organizing a Process Essay

Whether your essay is a process explanation or a set of instructions, you can either devote a full paragraph to each step of the process or group a series of minor steps together in a single paragraph.

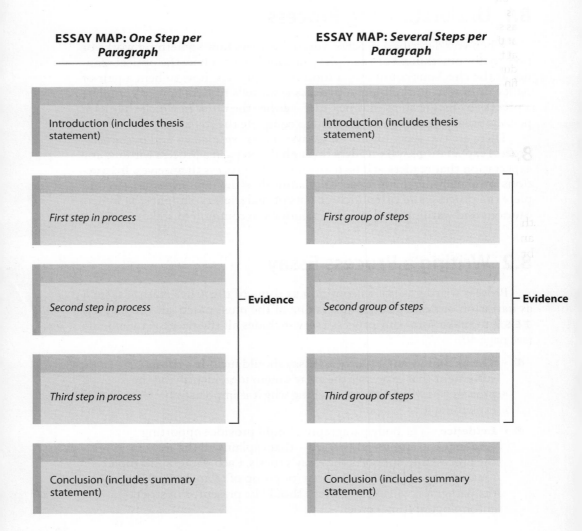

ESSAY MAP: *One Step per Paragraph*

Introduction (includes thesis statement)

First step in process

Second step in process ⎫
                         ⎬ Evidence
Third step in process   ⎭

Conclusion (includes summary statement)

ESSAY MAP: *Several Steps per Paragraph*

Introduction (includes thesis statement)

First group of steps

Second group of steps ⎫
                        ⎬ Evidence
Third group of steps   ⎭

Conclusion (includes summary statement)

As you write your process essay, discuss each step in the order in which it is performed, making sure your topic sentences clearly identify each step or group of steps. (If you are writing instructions, you may also include reminders or warnings that readers might need to know when performing the process.)

SOME TRANSITIONAL WORDS AND PHRASES FOR PROCESS

Transitions are very important in process essays. They enable readers to clearly identify each step — for example, *first*, *second*, *third*, and so on. In addition, they establish a sequence that lets readers move easily through the process you are describing.

after that,	first	subsequently
after this	immediately	the first (second,
as	later	third) step
as soon as	meanwhile	the next step
at the same time	next	the last step
at this point	now	then
during	once	when
finally	soon	while

8.4 Case Study: A Student Writes a Process Essay

Here is how one student, Melany Hunt, wrote a process essay in response to the assignment, "Write an essay explaining a process that changed your appearance in some way." To make sure she had enough to write about, she did some brainstorming, making the following list of possible steps she could include:

Decide to dye hair

Select hair dye color

Buy the hair dye

Try Veronica's house

Move everything to my house

Set up the bathroom

Read the instructions

Reconsider the whole plan

Buy hats

Use special conditioner

Wait for dye to set in

Rinse

Admire results

                    Mix dye tubes
                    Apply dye

After looking over her list, Melany crossed out steps she didn't think
were essential to the process she wanted to describe.

                    ~~Decide to dye hair~~
                    Select hair dye color
                    Buy the hair dye
                    ~~Try Veronica's house~~
                    ~~Move everything to my house~~
                    ~~Set up the bathroom~~
                    ~~Read the instructions~~
                    ~~Reconsider the whole plan~~
                    Buy hats
                    Use special conditioner
                    Wait for dye to set in
                    Rinse
                    ~~Admire results~~
                    Mix dye tubes
                    Apply dye

Once she had decided on her list of steps, Melany made an informal outline,
arranging the steps in the order in which they were performed.

                    Preparation
                        Select hair dye color
                        Buy the hair dye
                    The Process
                        Dye hair
                            Mix dye tubes
                            Apply dye
                            Wait for dye to set in
                            Use special conditioner
                        Rinse
                    The Result
                        Buy hats

Then, Melany wrote a first draft of her essay. She focused on getting her ideas
down on the page, knowing she would come back and revise her essay later
to make it stronger. Read through Melany's draft, and then answer the questions in the peer-editing worksheet on page 84.

Melany Hunt, First Draft:

Don't Do It

The beautiful woman pictured on the box seemed to beckon to me. I reached for the box of hair color. I can't remember my friend Veronica's and my reasons for wanting to change our hair color, but they seemed to make sense at the time. Maybe we were just bored. I do remember that the idea of transforming our appearance came up unexpectedly. We decided to change our hair color that very evening. The process that followed taught me that some impulses should definitely be resisted.

We decided to use my bathroom to color our hair. Inside each box of hair color, we found two little bottles and a small tube wrapped in a page of instructions. Attached to the instruction page itself were two very large plastic gloves, which looked and felt like plastic sandwich bags. After we put our gloves on, we began the actual coloring process. First we poured the first bottle into the second, which was half-full of some odd-smelling liquid.

The directions said to leave the color on the hair for fifteen to twenty minutes, so we found a little timer and set it for fifteen minutes. We then wrapped the old towels around our sour-smelling hair and went outside to get some fresh air.

The last part of the process involved applying the small tube of conditioner to our hair. We used the conditioner as directed, and then we dried our hair so that we could see the actual color.

Even before I looked in the mirror, I heard Veronica's gasp. I told her that I didn't think her joke was very funny and then complimented her on her own brand new hair color. It turned out, though, that she was serious. Something had gone wrong.

My hair was the putrid greenish-brown color of a winter lawn, dying in patches yet still a nice green in the shade.

The next day in school, I wore my hair tied back under a baseball cap. It is now three months later, and I still have no idea what prompted me to color my hair. I wish I hadn't done it, and all I can say is that I hope my hair grows out quickly!

---

1. What process does this essay describe?

2. Does the writer include all the information the audience needs? Is any vital step or piece of information missing? Is any step or piece of information irrelevant? Is any necessary definition, explanation, or caution missing or incomplete?

3. Is the essay a set of instructions or a process explanation? How can you tell? Why do you think the writer chose this strategy rather than the alternative? Do you think it was the right choice?

4. Does the writer consistently follow the stylistic conventions for the strategy — instructions or process explanation — the author has chosen?

5. Are the steps presented in a clear, logical order? Are they grouped logically into paragraphs? Should any steps be combined or relocated? If so, which ones?

6. Does the writer use enough transitions to move readers through the process? Should any transitions be added? If so, where?

7. Does the writer need to revise to correct confusing shifts in tense, person, voice, or mood? If so, where?

8. Is the essay interesting? What descriptive details would add interest to the essay? Would a visual be helpful?

9. How would you characterize the writer's opening strategy? Is it appropriate for the essay's purpose and audience? What alternative strategy might be more effective?

10. How would you characterize the writer's closing strategy? Would a different conclusion be more effective? Explain.

8.5 Analyzing a Process Essay

When Melany finished her revisions, she prepared a final draft. Read her final draft, and complete the practice exercise that follows it.

Medium Ash Brown

The beautiful chestnut-haired woman pictured on the box seemed to beckon to me. I reached for the box of Medium Ash Brown hair color just as my friend Veronica grabbed the box labeled Sparkling Sherry. I can't remember our reasons for wanting to change our hair color, but they seemed to make sense at the time. Maybe we were just bored. I do remember that the idea of transforming our appearance came up unexpectedly. Impulsively, we decided to change our hair color—and, we hoped, ourselves—that very evening. The process that followed taught me that some impulses should definitely be resisted.

We decided to use my bathroom to color our hair. Inside each box of hair color, we found two little bottles and a small tube wrapped in a page of instructions. Attached to the instruction page itself were two very large, one-size-fits-all plastic gloves, which looked and felt like plastic sandwich bags. The directions recommended having some old towels around to soak up any spills or drips that might occur. Under the sink we found some old, frayed towels that I figured my mom had forgotten about, and we spread them around the bathtub. After we put our gloves on, we began the actual coloring process. First we poured the first bottle into the second, which was half-full of some odd-smelling liquid. The smell was not much better after we combined the two bottles. The directions advised us to cut off a small section of hair to use as a sample. For some reason, we decided to skip this step.

At this point, Veronica and I took turns leaning over the tub to wet our hair for the color. The directions said to leave the color on the hair for fifteen to twenty minutes, so we found a little timer and set it for fifteen minutes. Next, we applied the color to our hair. Again, we took turns, squeezing the bottle in order to cover all our hair. We then wrapped the old towels around our sour-smelling hair and went outside to get some fresh air.

After the fifteen minutes were up, we rinsed our hair. According to the directions, we were to add a little water and scrub as if we were shampooing our hair. The color lathered up, and we rinsed our hair until the water ran clear. So far, so good.

The last part of the process involved applying the small tube of conditioner to our hair (because colored hair becomes brittle and easily damaged). We used the conditioner as directed, and then we dried our hair so that we could see the actual color.

Even before I looked in the mirror, I heard Veronica's gasp.

"Nice try," I said, assuming she was just trying to make me nervous, "but you're not funny."

"Mel," she said, "look in the mirror." Slowly, I turned around. My stomach turned into a lead ball when I saw my reflection. My hair was the putrid greenish-brown color of a winter lawn, dying in patches yet still a nice green in the shade.

The next day in school, I wore my hair tied back under a baseball cap. I told only my close friends what I had done. After they were finished laughing, they offered their deepest, most heartfelt condolences. They also offered many suggestions — none very helpful — on what to do to get my old hair color back.

It is now three months later, and I still have no idea what prompted me to color my hair. My only consolation is that I resisted my first impulse: to use a wild color, like blue or fuchsia. Still, as I wait for my hair to grow out, and as I assemble a larger and larger collection of baseball caps, it is small consolation indeed.

Practice: Analyzing a Process Essay

1. Underline the thesis statement. Then, restate it in your own words.

2. Is this a process explanation or instructions? How do you know?

3. List the steps in the process.

   _____

   _____

   _____

   _____

   _____

   _____

4. Circle the transitional words and phrases that Melany uses to move readers from one step to the next. Where, if anywhere, should more transitions be added?

5. Summarize the essay's conclusion in your own words.

6. **TEST** Melany's essay (see pages 79–80). Does she include all of the necessary elements?

7. What, specifically, did Melany change between her first and final drafts? Do you think all of Melany's changes improved her essay?

Cause and Effect

9.1 Understanding Cause and Effect

A **cause** is an event or situation that makes something else happen. An **effect** is a result of a particular cause or event. **Cause-and-effect essays** identify causes or predict effects, examining or analyzing the reasons and results. They also help readers to understand why something happened (or is happening) or how one event might affect another.

9.2 Writing a Cause-and-Effect Essay

When you **TEST** a cause-and-effect essay (see page 40), be sure that it includes the following elements:

- **T** • **Thesis Statement** — The introduction of a cause-and-effect essay should include a **thesis statement** that communicates the essay's main idea and indicates whether it will focus on causes or on effects.

- **E** • **Evidence** — The body paragraphs should include supporting **evidence** — examples and details — to illustrate and explain the causes or effects you examine. The topic sentence of each paragraph should identify the causes or effects the paragraph will discuss.

- **S** • **Summary Statement** — The conclusion of a cause-and-effect essay should include a **summary statement** that reinforces the essay's thesis.

- **T** • **Transitions** — A cause-and-effect essay should include **transitional words and phrases** that make clear which causes lead to which effects.

9.3 Organizing a Cause-and-Effect Essay

In the body of your essay, you will probably devote a full paragraph to each cause (or effect). You can also group several related causes (or effects) together in each paragraph.

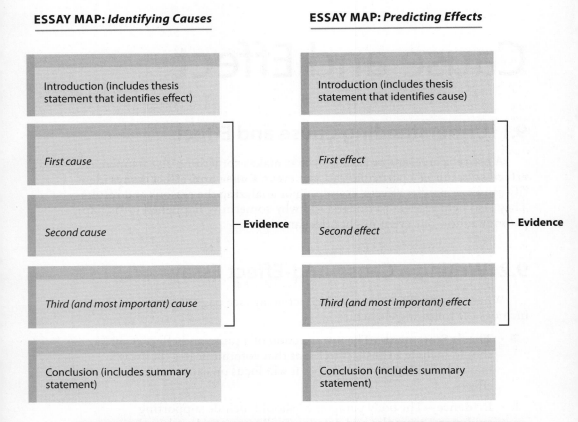

ESSAY MAP: *Identifying Causes*

Introduction (includes thesis statement that identifies effect)

First cause

Second cause ⎤
⎥ — **Evidence**
Third (and most important) cause ⎦

Conclusion (includes summary statement)

ESSAY MAP: *Predicting Effects*

Introduction (includes thesis statement that identifies cause)

First effect

Second effect ⎤
⎥ — **Evidence**
Third (and most important) effect ⎦

Conclusion (includes summary statement)

SOME TRANSITIONAL WORDS AND PHRASES FOR CAUSE AND EFFECT

Transitions in cause-and-effect essays introduce individual causes or effects. They may also show the connections between a cause and its effects or between an effect and its causes. In addition, they may indicate which cause or effect is more important than another.

accordingly	for this reason	third, final) effect
another cause	moreover	the first (second, third)
another effect	since	reason
as a result	so	the most important cause
because	the first (second,	the most important effect
consequently	third, final) cause	therefore
for	the first (second,	

9.4 Case Study: A Student Writes a Cause-and-Effect Essay

Here is how one student, Evelyn Pellicane, wrote a cause-and-effect essay as part of an in-class history exam. Before the exam, she took careful notes in her history class, which she studied in preparation for the test. Below are two excerpts from her class notes.

Date your notes. Instructors frequently identify material that will be on a test by dates. If you do not date your notes, you may not know exactly what to study.

Try to include an example for each important concept introduced in class — something that will help you remember what the instructor was talking about.

<u>Sept 20: Great Britain, Scotland, Ireland, and Wales, mid-1800's</u>

Whig govt in power in England (Whig = "protectionist in economic policy"). Moral reforms (Factory Act 1847, Public Health Act 1848), but economically conservative. Whigs believed in *laissez-faire* = as little government interference in economy as possible.

Scotland: tenants sent away by landowners and replaced by Cheviot sheep. Sheep made more money for landlords than having tenant farmers. Some landlords pay to help tenants immigrate to Canada, US, and AUS.

Imported into England: Cotton, oil, wheat, sugar, wool (Cheviot sheep), corn (Ireland).

****Exam on 1840's Europe — Oct 7!!!

<u>Sept 22: The Irish Potato Famine, 1845–1849</u>

Potato blight (fungus) in 1845, caused potatoes to rot in the ground. Potatoes were main food source (60%) for tenant-farmers in Ireland.

Corn Laws taxed import of grain to keep price of British corn high. Brits wouldn't repeal Corn Laws even with famine, so grain was too $$ to import to feed the Irish.

When you review your notes after class, write down any questions you want to ask the instructor at the top of the next blank page in your class notebook. When you begin your notes for the next class, your questions will be at the top as a useful reminder.

Immigration: Some landowners paid to help (like in Scotland). No education or skilled labor in many immigrants. Moved to slums in major cities — London, Glasgow, Quebec, New York, Boston — but hating the British. 1.5 <u>MILLION</u> left Ireland between 1845–1855 (~50 thous. a year).

Population of Ireland: 9 million down to 6½ million

**Question for Prof. Perez: Why did the British government collect taxes from Ireland during the famine?

Taking exams can be a stressful process. The tips in the box on the next page will help you prepare before an exam and stay on track during the exam itself.

TAKING EXAMS

Preparation for an exam should begin well before the exam is announced. In a sense, you begin this preparation on the first day of class.

Before the Exam

1. ***Attend every class.*** Regular attendance in class — where you can listen, ask questions, and take notes — is the best possible preparation for exams. If you do have to miss a class, arrange to copy — and read — another student's notes *before the next class* so you will be able to follow the discussion.

2. ***Keep up with the reading.*** Read every assignment, and read it before the class in which it will be discussed. If you do not, you may have trouble understanding what is going on in class.

3. ***Take careful notes.*** Take careful, thorough notes, but be selective. If you can, compare your notes on a regular basis with those of other students in the class; working together, you can fill in gaps or correct errors. Establishing a buddy system will also force you to review your notes regularly instead of just on the night before the exam.

4. ***Study on your own.*** When an exam is announced, adjust your study schedule — and your priorities — so you have time to review everything. (This is especially important if you have more than one exam in a short period of time.) Over a period of several days, review all your material (class notes, readings, and so on), and then review it again. Make a note of anything you do not understand, and keep track of topics you need to review. Try to predict the most likely questions, and — if you have time — practice answering them.

5. ***Study with a group.*** If you can, set up a study group. Studying with others can help you better understand the material. However, do not come to group sessions unprepared and expect to get all the information you need from the other students. You must first study on your own.

6. ***Make an appointment with your instructor.*** Make a conference appointment with the course instructor or teaching assistant a few days before the exam. Bring to this meeting any specific questions you have about course content and about the format of the upcoming exam. (Be sure to prepare for the conference by reviewing all your study material in advance.)

7. ***Review the material one last time.*** The night before the exam is not the time to begin your studying; it is the time to review. When you have finished your review, get a good night's sleep.

During the Exam

By the time you walk into the exam room, you will already have done all you could to get ready for the test. Your goal now is to keep the momentum going and not do anything to undermine all your hard work.

1. ***Read through the entire exam.*** Be sure you understand how much time you have, how many points each question is worth, and exactly what each

question is asking you to do. Many exam questions call for just a short answer — *yes* or *no*, *true* or *false*. Others ask you to fill in a blank with a few words, and still others require you to select the best answer from among several choices. If you are not absolutely certain what kind of answer a particular question calls for, ask the instructor or the proctor *before* you begin to write.

2. **Budget your time.** Once you understand how much each section of the exam and each question are worth, plan your time and set your priorities, devoting the most time to the most important questions. If you know you tend to rush through exams, or if you find you often run out of time before you get to the end of a test, you might try checking your progress when about one-third of the allotted time has passed (for a one-hour exam, check after twenty minutes) to make sure you are pacing yourself appropriately.

3. **Reread each question.** Carefully reread each question *before* you start to answer it. Underline the **keywords** — the words that give specific information about how to approach the question and how to phrase your answer. (These keywords are listed in the Reminder box on page 92.)

    Remember, even if everything you write is correct, your response is not acceptable if you do not answer the question. If a question asks you to compare two novels, writing a *summary* of one of them will not be acceptable.

4. **Brainstorm to help you recall the material.** If you are writing a paragraph or an essay, look frequently at the question as you brainstorm. Quickly write down all the relevant points you can think of — what the textbook had to say, your instructor's comments, and so on. The more information you can think of now, the more you will have to choose from when you write your answer.

5. **Write down the main idea.** Looking closely at the way the question is worded and at your brainstorming notes, write a sentence that states the main idea of your answer. If you are writing a paragraph, this sentence will be your **topic sentence**; if you are writing an essay, it will be your **thesis statement**.

6. **List your key supporting points.** You do not want to waste your limited (and valuable) time making a detailed outline, but an informal outline that lists just your key points is worth the little time it takes. An informal outline will help you plan a clear direction for your paragraph or essay.

7. **Draft your answer.** You will spend most of your time actually writing the answers to the questions on the exam. Follow your outline, keep track of time, and consult your brainstorming notes when you need to — but stay focused on your writing.

8. **Reread, revise, and edit.** When you have finished drafting your answer, reread it carefully to make sure it says everything you want it to say — and that it answers the exam question.

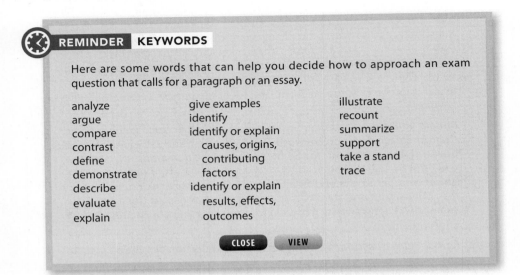

REMINDER   KEYWORDS

Here are some words that can help you decide how to approach an exam question that calls for a paragraph or an essay.

analyze	give examples	illustrate
argue	identify	recount
compare	identify or explain	summarize
contrast	causes, origins,	support
define	contributing	take a stand
demonstrate	factors	trace
describe	identify or explain	
evaluate	results, effects,	
explain	outcomes	

CLOSE   VIEW

Following the advice in the Taking Exams box on pages 90–91, Evelyn reviewed the exam question, looking for keywords that would help her decide what to write about and how to structure her essay.

Question: "The 1840's were volatile years in Europe. Choose one social, political, or economic event that occurred during those years, analyze its causes, and briefly note how the event influenced later developments in European history."

Because Evelyn had taken careful notes on the Irish famine in class, she chose to focus on this event in her essay. The keywords she identified in the exam question showed her that her material should be presented in a cause-and-effect essay. Once she decided on her essay's subject and structure, she went on to brainstorm, creating the chart below to help her keep track of the various causes and outcomes she planned to discuss in her essay.

Causes	*Effects*
Failure of the potato crop (multiple years)	Immediate cause. Potatoes rotted; Not enough potatoes to feed everyone; People eating weeds; People could not pay rent, were evicted.

Landlord-tenant system
  -no leases
  -threat of prison
  -provided money for passage to
   America
	Evictions; Prison; People forced to leave their land; People emigrating to America.

Causes	Effects
Errors in government policy -no more selling corn -would not send food to Ireland -did not offer other forms of aid	Unstable economy; Starvation; Demonstrations; No food to buy.
British prejudice	Causes errors in government policy; Did not teach Irish how to use the aid given; Forced additional taxes; Hatred of the British exported to America and Canada; Ireland neutral in WWII.

Using this chart as a guide, Evelyn wrote her essay.

9.5 Analyzing a Cause-and-Effect Essay

Read Evelyn's in-class essay, and then answer the questions in the peer-editing checklist on page 96.

The Irish Famine, 1845–1849

The Irish famine, which brought hardship and tragedy to Ireland during the 1840s, was caused and prolonged by four basic factors: the failure of the potato crop, the landlord-tenant system, errors in government policy, and the long-standing prejudice of the British toward Ireland.

The immediate cause of the famine was the failure of the potato crop. In 1845, potato disease struck the crop, and potatoes rotted in the ground. The 1846 crop also failed, and before long people were eating weeds. The 1847 crop was healthy, but there were not enough potatoes to go around, and in 1848 the blight struck again, leading to more and more evictions by landlords.

The tenants' position on the land had never been very secure. Most had no leases and could be turned out by their landlords at any time. If a tenant owed rent, he was evicted — or, worse, put in prison, leaving his family to starve. The threat of prison caused many tenants to leave their land; those who could leave Ireland did so, sometimes with money provided by their landlords. Some landlords did try to take care of their tenants, but most did not. Many were absentee landlords who spent their rent money abroad.

Government policy errors, although not an immediate cause of the famine, played an important role in creating an unstable economy and perpetuating starvation. In 1846, the government decided not to continue selling corn, as it had during the first year of the famine, claiming that low-cost purchases of corn by Ireland had paralyzed British trade by interfering with free enterprise. Therefore, 1846 saw a starving population, angry demonstrations, and panic; even those with money were unable to buy food. Still, the government insisted that if it sent food to Ireland, prices would rise in the rest of the United Kingdom and that this would be unfair to hardworking English and Scots. As a result, no food was sent. Throughout the years of the famine, the British government aggravated an already grave situation: they did nothing to improve agricultural operations, to help people adjust to another crop, to distribute seeds, or to reform the landlord-tenant system that made the tenants' position so insecure.

At the root of this poor government policy was the long-standing British prejudice against the Irish. Hostility between the two countries went back some six hundred years, and the British were simply not about to inconvenience themselves to save the Irish. When the Irish so desperately needed grain to replace the damaged potatoes, it was clear that grain had to be imported from England. This meant, however, that the Corn Laws, which had been enacted to keep the price of British corn high by taxing imported grain, had to be repealed. The British were unwilling to repeal the Corn Laws. Even when they did supply cornmeal, they made no attempt to explain to the Irish how to cook this unfamiliar food. Moreover, the British government was determined to make Ireland pay for its own poor, so it forced the collection of taxes. Since many landlords could not collect tax money, they were forced to evict their tenants. The British government's callous and indifferent treatment of the Irish has been called genocide.

As a result of this devastating famine, the population of Ireland was reduced from about nine million to about six and one-half million. During the famine years, men roamed the streets looking for work, begging when they found none. Epidemics of "famine fever" and dysentery reduced the population drastically. The most important historical result of the famine, however, was the massive immigration to the United States, Canada, and Great Britain of poor, unskilled people who had to struggle to fit into a skilled economy and who brought with them a deep-seated hatred of the British. (This same hatred remained strong in Ireland itself—so strong that during World War II, Ireland, then independent, remained neutral rather than coming to England's aid.) Irish immigrants faced slums, fever epidemics, joblessness, and hostility—even anti-Catholic laws and anti-Irish riots—in Boston, New York, London, Glasgow, and Quebec. In Ireland itself, poverty and discontent continued, and by 1848 those emigrating from Ireland included a more highly skilled class of farmers, the ones Ireland needed to recover and to survive.

The Irish famine, one of the great tragedies of the nineteenth century, was a natural disaster compounded by the insensitivity of the British government and the archaic agricultural system of Ireland. Although the deaths that resulted depleted Ireland's resources even more, the men and women who immigrated to other countries permanently enriched those nations.

Practice: Analyzing a Cause-and-Effect Essay

1. Underline Evelyn's thesis; then, restate it in your own words. Does this statement identify a cause or an effect?

2. Evelyn devotes much more attention to the causes of the famine than to the effects. Why? Was this a good decision?

3. Circle the transitional words and phrases Evelyn uses to make her cause-and-effect connections clear to her readers. Do you think she needs more of these transitions? If so, where?

4. Is Evelyn's straightforward title effective, or should she have used a more creative or eye-catching title? Can you suggest an alternative?

5. Summarize the essay's conclusion in your own words.

6. **T E S T** Evelyn's essay (see page 87). Does she include all of the necessary elements?

7. Because this was an in-class essay, Evelyn did not have time to write more than one draft. Use the peer-editing worksheet on the next page to suggest changes she might make if she were to revise.

PEER-EDITING WORKSHEET: CAUSE AND EFFECT

1. Paraphrase the essay's thesis. Is it explicitly stated? Should it be?

2. Does the essay focus on causes, effects, or both? Does the thesis statement clearly identify this focus? If not, how should the thesis statement be revised?

3. Does the writer consider *all* relevant causes or effects? Are any key causes or effects omitted? Are any irrelevant causes or effects included?

4. Make an informal outline of the essay. What determines the order of the causes or effects? Is this the most effective order? If not, what revisions do you suggest?

5. List the transitional words and phrases used to indicate causal connections. Are any additional transitions needed? If so, where?

6. Does the writer use *post hoc* reasoning? Point out any examples of illogical reasoning.

7. Are more examples or details needed to help readers understand causal connections? If so, where?

8. Do you find the writer's conclusions convincing? Why or why not?

9. Has the writer used any "the reason is because" constructions? If so, suggest revisions.

10. Are *affect* and *effect* used correctly? Point out any errors.

10

Comparison and Contrast

10.1 Understanding Comparison and Contrast

When you buy something — for example, a phone or a bike — you comparison-shop, looking at various models to determine how they are alike and how they are different. In other words, you *compare and contrast*. When you **compare**, you consider how things are similar. When you **contrast**, you consider how they are different. **Comparison-and-contrast essays** explain how two things are alike or how they are different; sometimes, they discuss both similarities and differences.

There are two kinds of comparison-and-contrast essays: *subject-by-subject* and *point-by-point*.

In a *subject-by-subject essay*, you divide your comparison into two parts and discuss one subject at a time. In the first half of your essay you discuss all the points about one subject, and in the second half you discuss all the points about the second subject. This approach is best for essays with a small number of points. If you discuss too many points, readers will have difficulty remembering them when you get to the second subject.

When you write a *point-by-point essay*, you discuss a point about one subject and then the same point about the second subject. You use this alternating pattern throughout your essay, typically discussing one point in each paragraph. This is a good strategy if you are comparing many points, or if your topic is technical or complicated. Because you compare the two subjects one point at a time, readers will be able to consider one point of comparison fully before moving on to the next point.

10.2 Writing a Comparison-and-Contrast Essay

Regardless of which organization you choose, you should discuss the same points in the same order for both of your subjects. In addition, use **TEST** to make sure that your comparison-and-contrast essay includes all the necessary elements (see page 40).

T • **Thesis Statement** — The introduction of a comparison-and-contrast essay should include a **thesis statement** that communicates the essay's main idea, telling readers what two items you are going to compare or contrast and whether you are going to emphasize similarities or differences.

E • **Evidence** — The body paragraphs should include supporting **evidence** — examples and details — that supports the thesis statement. The topic sentence of each paragraph should identify the similarity or difference the paragraph will examine, and the examples and details should explain the similarity or difference. Points should be arranged in a logical order — for example, from least to most important.

S • **Summary Statement** — The conclusion of a comparison-and-contrast essay should include a **summary statement** that reinforces the essay's thesis.

T • **Transitions** — A comparison-and-contrast essay should include **transitional words and phrases** to help readers move from point to point and from subject to subject.

10.3 Organizing a Comparison-and-Contrast Essay

When you organize a comparison-and-contrast essay, you can choose either a *point-by-point* or a *subject-by-subject* arrangement. A **point-by-point** comparison alternates between the two subjects you are comparing or contrasting, moving back and forth from one subject to the other. A **subject-by-subject** comparison treats its two subjects separately, first fully discussing one subject and then moving on to consider the other subject. In both kinds of comparison-and-contrast essays, the same points are discussed in the same order for both subjects.

ESSAY MAP: *Point-by-Point Comparison*

Introduction (thesis statement identifies subjects to be compared or contrasted)

First point discussed for both subjects

Second point discussed for both subjects

Third point discussed for both subjects

— **Evidence**

Conclusion (includes summary statement)

ESSAY MAP: *Subject-by-Subject Comparison*

Introduction (thesis statement identifies subjects to be compared or contrasted)

First subject discussed

First subject discussed

Second subject discussed

Second subject discussed

— **Evidence**

Conclusion (includes summary statement)

SOME TRANSITIONAL WORDS AND PHRASES FOR COMPARISON AND CONTRAST

Transitions make your essay more coherent by showing readers whether you are focusing on similarities (for example, *likewise* or *similarly*) or differences (for example, *although* or *in contrast*). Transitions also tell readers when you are changing from one point (or one subject) to another.

although	one difference . . . another difference
but	one similarity . . . another similarity
even though	on the contrary
however	on the one hand . . . on the other hand
in comparison	similarly
in contrast	though
like	unlike
likewise	whereas
nevertheless	

10.4 Case Study: A Student Writes a Comparison-and-Contrast Essay

Here is how one student, Mark Cotharn, wrote a comparison-and-contrast essay in response to the assignment, "Write an essay comparing two educational experiences." Knowing that he needed to address the same points for each of his subjects, he brainstormed with this structure in mind.

Old High School	New High School
Great football team	Poor football team
Sports = primary value	Academics = primary value
Town support	Town didn't care
Personal contact from coach	Limited contact from coach
Teachers treated as a friend	Teachers treated as potential problem
Teachers offered special treatment	Teachers were harder on me

After looking at his lists, Mark eliminated points he didn't need and arranged the rest into an informal outline.

Old high school
  Great football team
  Sports valued above everything
  Personal contact from coach
  Special treatment from teachers

New high school
    Poor football team
    Academics valued above everything
    Limited contact with coach
    No special treatment from teachers

After Mark completed his outline, he made sure that he had a clear thesis that conveyed his main idea. He then wrote his draft, focusing on the differences between the two schools he attended. Read through Mark's first draft, and then answer the questions in the peer-editing worksheet on page 103.

Mark Cotharn, First Draft

Brains versus Brawn

Discrimination can take a lot of forms. When I was a sophomore, I benefited from discrimination. When I was a junior, I was penalized by it, treated as if there were no place for me in a classroom. Both these types of discrimination are wrong.

At my high school, football was everything, and the entire town supported the local team. In the summer, merchants would run special football promotions, and everyone came to the games. Coming out of junior high school, I was considered a great athlete who was eventually going to start as varsity quarterback. Because of this, I was welcomed by the high school. Before I entered the school, the varsity coach visited my home, and the principal called my parents and told them how well I was going to do.

I knew that high school would be different from junior high, but I wasn't prepared for the treatment I received from my teachers. Many of them talked to me as if I were their friend, not their student. I only had one teacher who loved football, but still held me accountable. My history teacher always told me that he admired my skill, but talked to me about how important it was to develop as many skills as I could. The others, though, gave me a lot of special treatment. My math teacher used to keep me after class just to talk football. My biology teacher told me I could skip labs to give me time for myself before practice. Several of my teachers told me that during football season, I didn't have to hand in homework because it might distract me during practice. My Spanish teacher even told me that if I didn't do well on a test, I could take it over after the season. Everything I did seemed to be perfect.

Despite this favorable treatment, I continued to study. Just like my history teacher told me, I knew that if I wanted to go to a good college, I would have to get good grades. I also resented the idea that I could only get good grades if the teachers were helping me. I had always been a good student, and I had no intention of changing my study habits now that I was in high school. Each night after practice, I stayed up late making sure my homework was done. Any studying I couldn't do during the week, I would complete on the weekends. Of course, my social life suffered, but I didn't care. I was proud that I never took advantage of the special treatment my teachers were offering me. I think my history teacher was proud of me too.

Then, one day the township redrew the school-district lines, and I found myself assigned to a new high school — one that was a lot harder than the one I attended and, worse, one that had a weak football team. When my parents appealed to the school board to let me stay at my current school, they were told that if the board made an exception for me, it would have to make exceptions for others, and that would lead to chaos. My principal and my coach also tried to get the board to change its decision, but they got the same response. So, in my junior year, at the height of my career, I changed schools.

Unlike the people at my old school, no one at my new school seemed to care much about high school football. Many of the students attended the games, but their primary focus was on getting into college. If they talked about football at all, they usually discussed the regional college teams, so I didn't have the status I used to. When I met with the coach before school started, he told me the football team was weak. He also told me that his main goal was to make sure everyone on the team had a chance to play. So, even though I would start, I would have to share the quarterback position with two other seniors. Later that day, I saw the principal, who told me that although sports were an important part of school, academic achievement was more important. He threatened not to let me play if my grades were bad.

The teachers at my new school did not give any special treatment to athletes. When I entered my new school, I was ready for the challenge. What I was not ready for was the hostility of everyone. My teachers made it obvious that they had already made up their minds about what kind of student I was going to be. Some teachers told me I shouldn't expect any special consideration just because I was the team's quarterback. One even said in front of the class that I would have to study as hard as the other students if I expected to pass. I didn't expect anyone to give me anything, and I was ready to get the grades I deserved. After all, I had gotten good grades up to this point, and I had no reason to think that the situation would change. Even so, my teachers' attitudes upset me.

Just as I had in my old school, I studied hard, but I didn't know how to deal with the prejudice I faced. At first, it bothered me and even affected my performance on the football field. However, after a while, I decided that the best way to show my teachers that I was not just a jock was to prove to them what kind of student I really was. In the long run, far from discouraging me, their treatment motivated me, and I decided to work as hard in the classroom as I did on the football field. By the end of high school, not only had the team won half of its games, but I had also proved to my teachers that I was a good student.

As angry as I was at the teachers in my new school, my experience did have some positive effects. I learned that you should judge people on their merits, not by your own set of assumptions. I also learned that although some people are talented intellectually, others have special skills that should also be valued. Discriminatory treatment, whether it helps you or hurts you, is no substitute for fairness.

 PEER-EDITING WORKSHEET: COMPARISON AND CONTRAST

1. Does the essay have a clearly stated thesis? What is it?

2. What two things are being compared? What basis for comparison exists between the two?

3. Does the essay treat the same or similar points for each of its two subjects? List the points discussed.

FIRST SUBJECT	SECOND SUBJECT
a.	a.
b.	b.
c.	c.
d.	d.

   Are these points discussed in the same order for both subjects? Are the points presented in parallel terms?

4. Does the essay use a point-by-point or subject-by-subject strategy? Is this strategy the best choice? Why?

5. Are transitional words and phrases used appropriately to identify points of comparison and contrast? List some of the transitions used.

6. Are additional transitions needed? If so, where?

7. How could the introductory paragraph be improved?

8. How could the concluding paragraph be improved?

9. Does the writer use sources? Are they appropriate and helpful? Does the writer need to document sources?

10. Does the writer need to add a visual?

10.5 Analyzing a Comparison-and-Contrast Essay

When Mark finished his revisions, he prepared a final draft. Read his final draft, and then do the practice exercise that follows it.

Brains versus Brawn

When people think about discrimination, they usually associate it with race or gender. But discrimination can take other forms. For example, a person can gain an unfair advantage at a job interview by being attractive, by knowing someone who works at the company, or by being able to talk about something (like sports) that has nothing to do with the job. Certainly, the people who do not get the job would claim that they were discriminated against, and to some extent they would be right. As a high school athlete, I experienced both sides of discrimination. When I was a sophomore, I benefited from discrimination. When I was a junior, however, I was penalized by it, treated as if there were no place for me in a classroom. As a result, I learned that discrimination, whether it helps you or hurts you, is wrong.

At my first high school, football was everything, and the entire town supported the local team. In the summer, merchants would run special football promotions. Adults would wear shirts with the team's logo, students would collect money to buy equipment, and everyone would go to the games and cheer the team on. Coming out of junior high school, I was considered an exceptional athlete who was eventually going to start as varsity quarterback. Because of my status, I was enthusiastically welcomed by the high school. Before I entered the school, the varsity coach visited my home, and the principal called my parents and told them how well I was going to do.

I knew that high school would be different from junior high, but I wasn't prepared for the treatment I received from my teachers. Many of them talked to me as if I were their friend, not their student. My math teacher used to keep me after class just to talk football; he would give me a note so I could be late for my next class. My biology teacher told me I could skip the afternoon labs so that I would have some time for myself before practice. Several of my teachers told me that during football season, I didn't have to hand in homework because it might distract me during practice. My Spanish teacher even told me that if I didn't do well on a test, I could take it over after the season. Everything I did seemed to be perfect.

Despite this favorable treatment, I continued to study hard. I knew that if I wanted to go to a good college, I would have to get good grades, and I resented the implication that the only way I could get good grades was by getting special treatment. I had always been a good student, and I had no intention of changing my study habits now that I was in high school. Each night after practice, I stayed up late outlining my notes and completing my class assignments. Any studying I couldn't do during the week, I would complete on the weekends. Of course, my social life suffered, but I didn't care. I was proud that I never took advantage of the special treatment my teachers were offering me.

Then, one day, the unthinkable happened. The township redrew the school-district lines, and I suddenly found myself assigned to a new high school — one that was academically more demanding than the one I attended and, worse, one that had a weak football team. When my parents appealed to the school board to let me stay at my current school, they were told that if the board made an exception for me, it would have to make exceptions for others, and that would lead to chaos. My principal and my coach also tried to get the board to change its decision, but they got the same response. So, in my junior year, at the height of my career, I changed schools.

Unlike the people at my old school, no one at my new school seemed to care much about high school football. Many of the students attended the games, but their primary focus was on getting into college. If they talked about football at all, they usually discussed the regional college teams. As a result, I didn't have the status I had when I attended my former school. When I met with the coach before school started, he told me the football team was weak. He also told me that his main goal was to make sure everyone on the team had a chance to play. So, even though I would start, I would have to share the quarterback position with two seniors. Later that day, I saw the principal, who told me that although sports were an important part of school, academic achievement was more important. He made it clear that I would play football only as long as my grades did not suffer.

Unlike the teachers at my old school, the teachers at my new school did not give any special treatment to athletes. When I entered my new school, I was ready for the challenge. What I was not ready for was the hostility of most of my new teachers. From the first day, in just about every class, my teachers made it obvious that they had already made up their minds about what kind of student I was going to be. Some teachers told me I shouldn't expect any special consideration just because I was the team's quarterback. One even said in front of the class that I would have to study as hard as the other students if I expected to pass. I was hurt and embarrassed by these comments. I didn't expect anyone to give me anything, and I was ready to get the grades I deserved. After all, I had gotten good grades up to this point, and I had no reason to think that the situation would change. Even so, my teachers' preconceived ideas upset me.

Just as I had in my old school, I studied hard, but I didn't know how to deal with the prejudice I faced. At first, it really bothered me and even affected my performance on the football field. However, after a while, I decided that the best way to show my teachers that I was not the stereotypical jock was to prove to them what kind of student I really was. In the long run, far from discouraging me, their treatment motivated me, and I decided to work as hard in the classroom as I did on the football field. By the end of high school, not only had the team won half of its games (a record season), but I had also proved to my teachers that I was a good student. (I still remember the surprised look on the face of my chemistry teacher when she handed my first exam back to me and told me that I had received the second-highest grade in the class.)

Before I graduated, I talked to the teachers about how they had treated me during my junior year. Some admitted they had been harder on me than on the rest of the students, but others denied they had ever discriminated against me. Eventually, I realized that some of them would never understand what they had done. Even so, my experience did have some positive effects. I learned that you should judge people on their merits, not by your own set of assumptions. In addition, I learned that although some people are talented intellectually, others have special skills that should also be valued. And, as I found out, discriminatory treatment, whether it helps you or hurts you, is no substitute for fairness.

Practice: Analyzing a Comparison-and-Contrast Essay

1. Restate Mark's thesis in your own words.

2. Does Mark's opening paragraph identify the subjects he will discuss? Does it tell whether he will focus on similarities or on differences?

3. Mark's essay is a subject-by-subject comparison. What are his two subjects?

4. What is the purpose of paragraph 5?

5. Circle the transitional words and phrases the writer uses to move from one comparison to the next. Do you think these transitions are effective, or should they be revised to make the subject and points of comparison clearer?

6. **TEST** Mark's essay (see page 98). Does he include all of the necessary elements?

7. What, specifically, did Mark change between his first and final drafts? Do you think all of Mark's changes improved his essay?

Classification and Division

11.1 Understanding Classification and Division

When you **divide**, you take a whole (for instance, the contents of your laundry hamper) and break it into its individual parts. Each individual item of clothing is a part of the whole. When you **classify**, you sort items (people, things, ideas) into categories or groups. You classify when you sort the clothes from your hamper into piles of socks, T-shirts, jeans, and so on.

In a **classification-and-division essay**, you divide a whole (your subject) into parts and sort those parts or items into categories. Each category must be *distinct*. In other words, none of the items in one category should also fit into another category.

11.2 Writing a Classification-and-Division Essay

Along with identifying and explaining your categories, your classification-and-division essay should show readers how these categories are related to one another and why they are meaningful. You can **TEST** your classification-and-division essay to make sure it includes all the necessary elements (see page 40).

T · **Thesis Statement** — The introduction of a classification-and-division essay should include a **thesis statement** that communicates the essay's main idea and indicates what the essay's subject is and which categories will be used to classify it.

E • **Evidence** — The body paragraphs should provide **evidence** — examples and details — to support the thesis statement. The topic sentence of each paragraph should identify the category it will discuss, and the examples and details should explain the category and differentiate it from other categories. The categories should be arranged in **logical** order — for example, from least to most important or from smallest to largest.

S • **Summary Statement** — The conclusion of a classification-and-division essay should include a **summary statement** that reinforces the essay's thesis.

T • **Transitions** — A classification-and-division essay should include **transitional words and phrases** to show how categories are related to one another and to the thesis.

11.3 Organizing a Classification-and-Division Essay

As a rule, each paragraph of a classification-and-division essay examines a separate category — a different part of the whole. For example, a paragraph could focus on one kind of course in the college curriculum, one component of the blood, or one type of child. Within each paragraph, you discuss the individual items that you have put into a particular category — for example, accounting courses, red blood cells, or gifted students. If you consider some categories less important than others, you may decide to discuss those minor categories together in a single paragraph, devoting full paragraphs only to the most significant categories.

SOME TRANSITIONAL WORDS AND PHRASES FOR CLASSIFICATION AND DIVISION

Transitions tell readers when you are moving from one category to another (for example, *the first type, the second type*). They can also indicate which categories you think are more important than others (for example, *the most important, the least important*).

one kind . . . another kind	the first group . . . the last group
one way . . . another way	the first type . . . the second type
the first (second, third) category	the most (or least) important group
	the next part

ESSAY MAP: *One Category in Each Paragraph*

Introduction (thesis statement identifies whole and its major categories)

First category

Second category

Third category

⎤
⎥ — **Evidence**
⎦

Conclusion (includes summary statement)

ESSAY MAP: *Major Categories in Separate Paragraphs; Minor Categories Grouped Together*

Introduction (thesis statement identifies whole and its major categories)

Minor categories

First major category

Second (and more important) major category

⎤
⎥ — **Evidence**
⎦

Conclusion (includes summary statement)

11.4 Case Study: A Student Writes a Classification-and-Division Essay

Here is how one student, Josie Martinez, wrote a classification-and-division essay in response to the assignment, "Using Leon Wieseltier's 'Perhaps Culture Is Now the Counterculture' as your inspiration, look back at your own education and consider what you have learned so far."

She began by doing some brainstorming, considering all of the ways she could break down her subject (what she had learned) into categories.

Looking over her brainstorming, Josie realized that she had the most ideas about her actual classes, so she decided to write her essay about the different types of classes she had taken so far in college. To identify these different types of classes, she tried making a list.

Types of College Classes
Hard
Easy
Boring
Interesting
Surprising
Awesome
A waste of time
Fun
Useful

Although Josie did not find the list she generated very helpful, it did show her that some of the categories she had identified were too general or overlapped with other categories. (For example, a course could be both "easy" and "fun" or both "boring" and "a waste of time.") To create a more logical structure for her essay, Josie rethought her classification and came up with four distinct categories.

Rather than creating an informal outline at this point, Josie visually arranged her four categories in a chart, giving each category a descriptive title and including a specific course to illustrate each kind of class. When she wrote her first draft, she used each box in the chart as a paragraph.

Completely Awesome Shakespeare — great prof, great classmates, great subject	Completely Useless Movement Education — children's games were boring, no other content, threw away my notes
Seemed Good, but Useless Astronomy — love space, but we barely looked at the sky, only studied solar system, too much useless math	Seemed Useless, but Good Religion — had studied it all before, but lots of great history, meanings of languages, helped me put earlier knowledge into context

Using her chart as a guide, Josie wrote a first draft of her essay. At this point, she focused on her essay's organization, knowing she would come back and revise her essay later to add additional details. Read Josie's draft, and then answer the questions in the peer-editing worksheet on page 114.

Josie Martinez, First Draft

The Best and Worst College Classes

In "Perhaps Culture Is Now the Counterculture," Leon Wieseltier asks, "Has there ever been a moment in American life when the humanities were cherished less, and . . . needed more?" His essay goes on to stress the importance of balancing science and technology with humanities. Even though not every class will be rewarding or even enjoyable, taking a variety of courses in different disciplines will expose students to a wide range of subjects.

Most college classes can be classified into one of four categories. First are courses that students love — ideal learning environments where students would not change a thing. Far from these ideal courses are the completely worthless ones. Somewhere between these two extremes are two kinds of courses that are another pair of opposites: courses that students expect to enjoy, but that turn out to be completely disappointing and courses that students are initially not interested in but that exceed their expectations. Understanding these four categories can help students accept the fact that one disappointing class is not a disaster and can encourage them to try classes in different disciplines as well as those with different instructors and formats.

One of the best courses I ever took was my Shakespeare class. The professor who taught it had a great sense of humor and let anything go in her classroom. The students in the class shared an enthusiasm for Shakespeare, and they were eager to engage in lively discussions. This class gave us a thorough knowledge of Shakespeare's plays (tragedies, histories, comedies) as well as an understanding of his life. We also developed our analytical skills through our discussions of the plays and films as well as through special projects — for example, a character profile presentation and an abstract art presentation relating a work of art to one of the plays. This class was an ideal learning environment.

One of the most worthless courses I have taken in college was Movement Education. As an education major, I expected to like this class, and several other students who had taken it told me it was both easy and enjoyable. The class consisted of playing children's games and learning what made certain activities appropriate and inappropriate for children of various ages. Unfortunately, I never really enjoyed the games we played, and all of my notes were about these boring games I never wanted to use again — and I certainly didn't want to inflict them on a bunch of kids!

Although I looked forward to taking Introduction to Astronomy, I was very disappointed in this class. I had hoped to learn about the universe outside our solar system, but the instructor devoted most of the semester to our own solar system. In addition, a large part of our work included charting orbits and processing distance equations — work that I found both difficult and boring. Furthermore, we spent hardly any class time learning how to use a telescope and how to locate objects in the sky. In short, I gained little information from the class, learning only how to solve equations I would never use again and how to chart orbits that had already been charted.

I also took a religion class called Paul and the Early Church that was much better than I had anticipated. I attended Catholic school for thirteen years, so I assumed this course would offer me little that was new to me. However, because the class took a historical approach to studying Paul's biblical texts, I found that I learned more about Christianity than I had before. We learned about the historical validity of Paul and other texts in the Bible and how they were derived from various sources and passed orally through several generations before being written down and translated. This class was unlike any of my other religion classes — it was a complete surprise, but a really wonderful class.

Although each student's classes in college will be different — because every student has a different learning style, is interested in different subjects, and takes courses at different schools taught by different professors — all college students' experiences are similar in one respect. All students will encounter the same four kinds of courses: ideal, worthless, worse than expected, and better than expected. Understanding that these categories exist is important because it gives students the freedom and courage to try new things, as college students did years ago. Colleges used to be much better at encouraging students to try new things, before they became increasingly focused on what career people would have when they graduated. This new focus really hurts students today. After all, even if one course is a disappointment, another may be more interesting — or even exciting. For this reason, college students should not be discouraged by a course they do not like; the best classes are almost certainly still in their future.

Work Cited

Wieseltier, Leon. "Perhaps Culture Is Now the Counterculture: A Defense of the Humanities." *New Republic*, 28 May 2013. Newrepublic.com/article/113299/leon-wiseltier-commencement-speech-bradeis-university-2013

PEER-EDITING WORKSHEET: CLASSIFICATION AND DIVISION

1. Paraphrase the essay's thesis.

2. What whole is being divided into parts in this essay? Into what general categories is the whole divided?

3. Is each category clearly identified and explained? If not, what revisions can you suggest? (For example, can you suggest a different title for a particular category? A different topic sentence to introduce it?)

4. Where does the writer list the categories to be discussed? Is the list introduced by a colon (preceded by a complete sentence)? If not, suggest revisions.

5. Are the categories arranged in a logical order, one that indicates their relationships to one another and their relative importance? If not, how could they be rearranged?

6. Does the writer treat all relevant categories and no irrelevant ones? Which categories, if any, should be added, deleted, or combined?

7. Does the writer include all necessary items, and no unnecessary ones, within each category? What additional items could be added? Should any items be located elsewhere?

8. Does the writer treat all categories similarly, discussing comparable points for each? Should any additional points be discussed? If so, where?

9. Do topic sentences clearly signal the movement from one category to the next? Should any topic sentences be strengthened to mark the boundaries between categories more clearly? If so, which ones?

10. Could the writer use another pattern of development to structure this essay, or is classification and division the best choice? Explain.

11. Should the writer have added references to one or more sources?

12. Should the writer have added a visual?

11.5 Analyzing a Classification-and-Division Essay

When Josie finished her revisions, she prepared a final draft. Read her final draft, and then do the practice exercise that follows it.

What I Learned (and Didn't Learn) in College

In "Perhaps Culture Is Now the Counterculture," Leon Wieseltier writes in defense of the humanities, asking, "Has there ever been a moment in American life when the humanities were cherished less, and . . . needed more?" His essay goes on to stress the importance of balancing science and technology courses (increasingly popular with today's students) with humanities courses. Even though not every class will be rewarding or even enjoyable, taking a variety of courses in different disciplines will expose students to a wide range of subjects — and also teach them about themselves.

Despite the variety of experiences that different students have with different courses, most college classes can be classified into one of four categories: ideal classes, worthless classes, disappointing classes, and unexpectedly valuable classes. First are courses that students love — ideal learning environments in which they enjoy both the subject matter and the professor-student interaction. Far from these ideal courses are those that students find completely worthless in terms of subject matter, atmosphere, and teaching style. Somewhere between these two extremes are two kinds of courses that can be classified into another pair of opposites: courses that students expect to enjoy and to learn much from but are disappointing and courses that students are initially not interested in but that exceed their expectations. Understanding these four categories can help students accept the fact that one disappointing class is not a disaster and can encourage them to try classes in different disciplines as well as those with different instructors and formats.

One of the best courses I have taken so far as a college student was my Shakespeare class. The professor who taught it had a great sense of humor and was liberal in terms of what she allowed in her classroom — for example, controversial Shakespeare adaptations and virtually any discussion, relevant or irrelevant. The students in the class — English majors and non-English majors, those who were interested in the play as theater and those who preferred to study them as literature — shared an enthusiasm for Shakespeare, and they were eager to engage in lively discussions. This class gave us a thorough knowledge of Shakespeare's plays (tragedies, histories, comedies) as well as an understanding of his life. We also developed our analytical skills through our discussions of the plays and films as well as through special projects — for example, a character profile presentation and an abstract art presentation relating a work of art to one of the plays. This class was an ideal learning environment not only because of the wealth of material we were exposed to but also because of the respect with which our professor treated us: we were her colleagues, and she was as willing to learn from us as we were to learn from her.

In contrast to this ideal class, one of the most worthless courses I have taken in college was Movement Education. As an

education major, I expected to like this class, and several other
students who had taken it told me it was both easy and enjoyable.
The class consisted of playing children's games and learning what
made certain activities appropriate and inappropriate for children
of various ages. The only requirement for this class was that we had
to write note cards explaining how to play each game so that we
could use them for reference in our future teaching experiences.
Unfortunately, I never really enjoyed the games we played, and I have
long since discarded my note cards and forgotten how to play the
games — or even what they were.

Although I looked forward to taking Introduction to Astronomy,
I was very disappointed in this class. I had hoped to satisfy my
curiosity about the universe outside our solar system, but the
instructor devoted most of the semester to a detailed study of the
Earth and the other bodies in our own solar system. In addition, a
large part of our work included charting orbits and processing distance
equations — work that I found both difficult and boring. Furthermore,
we spent hardly any class time learning how to use a telescope and
how to locate objects in the sky. In short, I gained little information
from the class, learning only how to solve equations I would never
confront again and how to chart orbits that had already been charted.

In direct contrast to my astronomy class, a religion class called
Paul and the Early Church was much more rewarding than I had
anticipated. Having attended Catholic school for thirteen years, I
assumed this course would offer me little that was new to me. However,
because the class took a historical approach to studying Paul's biblical
texts, I found that I learned more about Christianity than I had in all
my previous religion classes. We learned about the historical validity
of Paul and other texts in the Bible and how they were derived from
various sources and passed orally through several generations before
being written down and translated into different languages. We
approached the texts from a linguistic perspective, determining the
significance of certain words and learning how various meanings can
be derived from different translations of the same passage. This class
was unlike any of my other religion classes in that it encouraged me
to study the texts objectively, leaving me with a new and valuable
understanding of material I had been exposed to for most of my life.

Although each student's learning experiences in college will
be different — because every student has a different learning style, is
interested in different subjects, and takes courses at different schools

taught by different professors—all college students' experiences are similar in one respect. All students will encounter the same kinds of courses: those that are ideal, those that are worthless, those that they learn little from despite their interest in the subject, and those that they learn from and become engaged in despite their low expectations. Understanding that these categories exist is important because it gives students the freedom and courage to try new things, as college students did years ago. After all, even if one course is a disappointment, another may be more interesting—or even exciting. For this reason, college students should not be discouraged by a course they do not like; the best classes are almost certainly still in their future.

Work Cited

Wieseltier, Leon. "Perhaps Culture Is Now the Counterculture: A Defense of the Humanities." *New Republic.* 28 May 2013. Newrepublic.com/article/113299/leon-wiseltier-commencement-speech-bradeis-university-2013

Practice: Analyzing a Classification-and-Division Essay

1. Restate Josie's thesis in your own words.

2. What four categories does Josie describe?

3. Is Josie's treatment of the four categories balanced? Does she present the same kind of information for each kind of college class?

4. How do Josie's topic sentences move readers from one category to the next? How do they link the four categories?

5. Do you think Josie should have included any additional categories? Should she have included fewer? Do any of her categories seem to overlap?

6. **TEST** Josie's essay (see pages 107–108). Does she include all of the necessary elements?

7. What, specifically, did Josie change between her first and final drafts? Do you think all of her changes improved her essay?

Definition

12.1 Understanding Definition

A **Definition** explains the meaning of a term or concept. In a history paper, for example, you might have to define *imperialism*, and in a book review you might need to explain why a novel is considered not science fiction but *steampunk*. When you want your audience to know exactly how you are using a specific term, you need to define it.

When most people think of definitions, they think of the *formal definitions* they see in a dictionary. Formal definitions, usually brief and to the point, can appear in an essay structured according to any pattern discussed in this textbook — for example, exemplification or narration. However, when you write an entire essay structured as a definition, you are creating an *extended definition*, a more complex and thorough explanation of what a person, place, or thing *is* or *means*.

12.2 Writing a Definition Essay

Extended definition essays do not follow a set pattern of development. Rather, they incorporate various patterns and strategies to help explain a term's meaning. **T E S T**ing your definition essays will help you to see if you have included all of the necessary elements (see page 40).

T • **Thesis Statement** — The introduction of a definition essay should include a **thesis statement** that communicates the essay's main idea and identifies the term you are going to define.

E • **Evidence** — The body paragraphs should include **evidence** — examples and details — that supports the thesis statement and defines your term. Body paragraphs may use different patterns of development, so be sure to use supporting evidence that is appropriate for the pattern of development you use.

S • **Summary Statement** — The conclusion of a definition essay should include a **summary statement** that reinforces the essay's thesis.

T • **Transitions** — A definition essay should include **transitional words and phrases** to move readers from one section of the definition to the next. You should choose transitions that are appropriate for the pattern or patterns of development that you use.

12.3 Organizing a Definition Essay

Definition essays can be developed in various ways. For example, you can define something by telling how it occurred (narration), by describing its appearance (description), by giving a series of examples (exemplification), by telling how it operates (process), by telling how it is similar to or different from something else (comparison and contrast), or by discussing its parts (classification).

Some definition essays use a single pattern of development; others combine several patterns of development, perhaps using a different one in each paragraph.

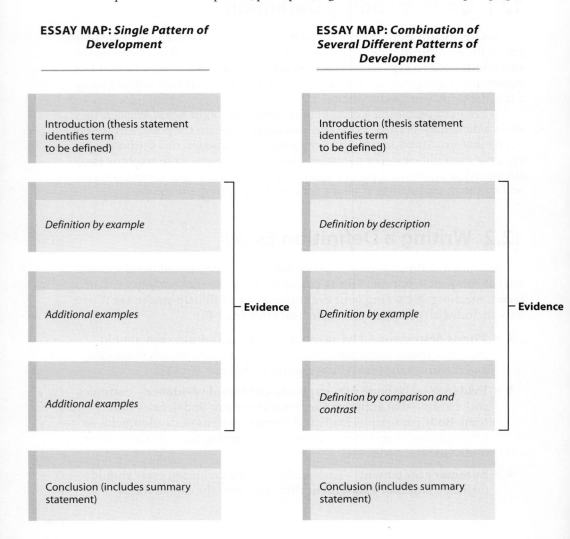

ESSAY MAP: *Single Pattern of Development*

Introduction (thesis statement identifies term to be defined)

Definition by example

Additional examples ⎤
                    ⎥— **Evidence**
Additional examples ⎦

Conclusion (includes summary statement)

ESSAY MAP: *Combination of Several Different Patterns of Development*

Introduction (thesis statement identifies term to be defined)

Definition by description

Definition by example ⎤
                      ⎥— **Evidence**
Definition by comparison and contrast ⎦

Conclusion (includes summary statement)

SOME TRANSITIONAL WORDS AND PHRASES FOR DEFINITIONS

Transitions are important for definition essays. They can signal moves from one narrative event to another. Transitions can also introduce examples.

also

for example

for men (for women)

however

in addition

in particular

in the 1990s (or another time)

like

often

one characteristic . . . another
 characteristic

one way . . . another way

sometimes

specifically

the first kind . . . the second kind

until recently

12.4 Case Study: A Student Writes a Definition Essay

Here is how one student, Ajoy Mahtab, wrote a definition essay in response to the assignment, "Write an extended definition of a term you assume is unfamiliar to your audience." Ajoy, who spent his childhood in India, decided to define *untouchable*, a term familiar to his family but unlikely to be understood by his classmates. To make sure that he had a clear understanding of the term he planned to define, he decided to begin by consulting a dictionary definition. When he looked up the word "untouchable," he discovered that it had two different meanings:

1. someone or something that is not able or allowed to be touched or otherwise impacted.

2. someone belonging to the lowest-caste of the Hindu caste system, or a person considered to be outside of that caste system.

Ajoy wanted to focus on the second definition, but he felt that his instructor and classmates might understand his term better if he explained how the caste system also related to the first definition, someone who was not allowed to be touched.

Next, Ajoy considered his approach to the essay and thought about what other patterns and strategies he could use to support his definition. He considered using **process** or **cause and effect** to explain the development of the caste system over many generations in India, but he finally decided to rely primarily on **classification and division** (to explain the caste system) and on **exemplification** and **narration** (to help his readers identify with the untouchables and understand their problems). He also included a formal definition.

After brainstorming to find ideas to write about, Ajoy made the following informal outline to keep himself on track as he wrote his first draft.

Introduction: Untouchable definition, India vs. the U.S.A.

Paragraph One: Explanation of caste system in India

Paragraph Two: How the caste system has changed over time

Paragraph Three: Explanation of Untouchables (put real definition here)

Paragraph Four: Festival story = evidence that untouchables still exist in Indian culture

Paragraph Five: Larger cultural evidence of untouchables and caste system

Paragraph Six: Argument: why this definition is harmful

Conclusion: The concept of someone as "untouchable" is hurtful and not right

Ajoy Mahtab, First Draft

The Untouchable

A word that is extremely common in India yet uncommon in the West is the word *untouchable*. In the West, it is generally used as a complimentary term. For example, an avid fan might say of an athlete, "He was absolutely untouchable. Nobody could even begin to compare with him." It seems rather ironic that a word could be so favorable in one culture and so negative in another. In India, however, the word takes on its more traditional definition, the one you would find in a dictionary: "that which cannot or should not be touched."

A caste system has traditionally existed in Indian society. At the top of the social ladder sat the Brahmins, or priests. Below them came the Kshatriyas, or the warrior caste. This caste included kings and nobles. Third on the social ladder were the Vaishyas, or merchants. Trade was their only form of livelihood. Last came the Shudras — the menials. Shudras were employed by the prosperous as sweepers and laborers.

Originally a person's caste was determined only by his profession. Thus, if the son of a merchant joined the army, he automatically converted from a Vaishya to a Kshatriya. However, the system soon became hereditary and rigid. Whatever one's occupation, one's caste was determined from birth according to the caste of one's father.

Outside of this structure were the untouchables, or Achhoots, people treated exactly like the dictionary definition of the word: a group of people shunned far more than lepers, people who were not considered even human. The untouchables of a village lived in a separate community downwind. They had a separate water supply, because they made the water impure if they were to drink from it. When they walked, they were made to bang two sticks together continuously so that passersby could hear them coming and thus avoid an untouchable's shadow. Tied to their waists, trailing behind them, was a broom that would clean the ground they had walked on. The penalty for not following these or any other rules was death for the untouchable or even the entire untouchable community.

Because of the efforts of great leaders like Mahatma Gandhi, untouchability is no longer anything like what it was. In India today, recognition of untouchability is punishable by law. Theoretically, there is no such thing as untouchability any more, but I know first-hand that it is a tradition that lingers on. I remember an incident from my childhood. I could not have been more than eight or nine at the time. I was on a holiday staying at my family's house. A festival was going on, and we were giving the servants small presents. I was handing them out when an old lady, bent with age, slowly hobbled into the room. When the entire line ended, she stepped hesitantly forward and stood in front of me, looking down at the ground. She then held a cloth stretched out in front of her. I was a little confused about how I was supposed to hand her the present, since both her hands were holding the cloth. Then, I learned that I was supposed to drop the gift into the cloth without touching the cloth itself. It was only later that I found out that she was an untouchable. This was the first time I had actually come face to face with such prejudice. That incident was burned into my memory, and I do not think I will ever forget it.

Even today, caste is an important factor in most marriages in India. Most Indian surnames reveal a person's caste immediately, so it is a difficult thing to hide. The shunning of the untouchable is more prevalent in South India, where people are much more devout than in the North. Some people would rather starve than share food and water with an untouchable. This concept is very difficult to accept in the West, but it is true all the same.

Why does a word that gives happiness in one part of the world cause pain in another? Why does the same word have different meanings to different people around the globe? Why do certain words cause rifts and others forge bonds? I do not think anyone can tell me the answers to these questions.

No actual parallel can be found today that compares to the horrors of untouchability. For an untouchable, life itself was a crime. The day was spent just trying to stay alive. From the misery of the untouchables, the world should learn a lesson: isolating and punishing any group of people is dehumanizing and immoral.

PEER-EDITING WORKSHEET: **DEFINITION**

1. What term is the writer defining? Does the essay include a formal definition of that term? If so, where? If no formal definition is included, should one be added?

2. For what purpose is the writer defining the term? Does the essay include a thesis statement that makes this purpose clear? If not, suggest revisions.

3. What patterns does the writer use to develop the definition? What other patterns could be used? Would a visual be helpful?

4. Does the writer use analogies to develop the definition? If so, where? Do you find these analogies helpful? What additional analogies might help readers understand the term more fully?

5. Does the essay define the term in language appropriate for its audience?

6. Does the writer use synonyms to develop the definition? If so, where? If not, where could synonyms be used to help communicate the term's meaning?

7. Does the writer use negation to develop the definition? If so, where? If not, could the writer strengthen the definition by explaining what the term is *not*?

8. Does the writer use enumeration to develop the definition? If so, where? If not, where in the essay might the writer list the term's special characteristics?

9. Does the writer explain the term's origin and development? If so, where? If not, do you believe this information should be added?

10. Reread the essay's introduction. If the writer uses a formal definition as an opening strategy, try to suggest an alternative opening.

12.5 Analyzing a Definition Essay

When Ajoy finished his revisions, he prepared a final draft. Read his final draft, and then do the practice exercise that follows it.

The Untouchable

A word that is extremely common in India yet uncommon to the point of incomprehension in the West is the word *untouchable*. It is a word that has had very sinister connotations throughout

India's history. A rigorously worked-out caste system has traditionally existed in Indian society. At the top of the social ladder sat the Brahmins, the class of the priesthood. These people had renounced the material world for a spiritual one. Below them came the Kshatriyas, or the warrior caste. This caste included the kings and all their nobles along with their armies. Third on the social ladder were the Vaishyas, who were the merchants of the land. Trade was their only form of livelihood. Last came the Shudras — the menials. Shudras were employed by the prosperous as sweepers and laborers. Originally a person's caste was determined only by his profession. Thus, if the son of a merchant joined the army, he automatically converted from a Vaishya to a Kshatriya. However, the system soon became hereditary and rigid. Whatever one's occupation, one's caste was determined from birth according to the caste of one's father.

Outside of this structure were a group of people, human beings treated worse than dogs and shunned far more than lepers, people who were not considered even human, people who defiled with their very touch. These were the Achhoots: the untouchables. The word *untouchable* is commonly defined as "that which cannot or should not be touched." In India, however, it was taken to a far greater extreme. The untouchables of a village lived in a separate community downwind of the borders of the village. They had a separate water supply, for they would make the village water impure if they were to drink from it. When they walked, they were made to bang two sticks together continuously so that passersby could hear them coming and thus avoid an untouchable's shadow. Tied to their waists, trailing behind them, was a broom that would clean the ground they had walked on. The penalty for not following these or any other rules was death for the untouchable and, in many instances, for the entire untouchable community.

One of the pioneers of the fight against untouchability was Mahatma Gandhi. Thanks to his efforts and those of many others, untouchability no longer presents anything like the horrific picture described above. In India today, in fact, recognition of untouchability is punishable by law. Theoretically, there is no such thing as untouchability any more. But old traditions linger on, and a deep-rooted fear passed down from generation to generation does not disappear overnight. Even today, caste is an important factor in most marriages. Most Indian surnames reveal a person's caste immediately, so it is a difficult thing to hide. The shunning of the untouchable is more prevalent in South India, where people are much more devout, than in the North. Some people would rather starve than share food and water with an untouchable. This concept is very difficult to accept in the West, but it is true all the same.

I remember an incident from my childhood. I could not have been more than eight or nine at the time. I was on a holiday staying at my family's house on the river Ganges. A festival was going on, and, as is customary, we were giving the servants small presents. I was handing them out when an old woman, bent with age, slowly hobbled into the room. She stood in the far corner of the room all alone, and no one so much as looked at her. When the entire line ended, she stepped hesitantly forward and stood in front of me, looking down at the ground. She then held a cloth stretched out in front of her. I was a little confused about how I was supposed to hand her the present, since both her hands were holding the cloth. Then, with the help of prompting from someone behind me, I learned that I was supposed to drop the gift into the cloth without touching the cloth itself. It was only later that I found out that she was an untouchable. This was the first time I had actually come face to face with such prejudice, and it felt like a slap in the face. That incident was burned into my memory, and I do not think I will ever forget it.

The word *untouchable* is not often used in the West, and when it is, it is generally used as a complimentary term. For example, an avid fan might say of an athlete, "He was absolutely untouchable. Nobody could even begin to compare with him." It seems rather ironic that a word could be so favorable in one culture and so negative in another. Why does a word that gives happiness in one part of the world cause pain in another? Why does the same word have different meanings to different people around the globe? Why do certain words cause rifts and others forge bonds? I do not think anyone can tell me the answers to these questions.

No actual parallel can be found today that compares to the horrors of untouchability. For an untouchable, life itself was a crime. The day was spent just trying to stay alive. From the misery of the untouchables, the world should learn a lesson: isolating and punishing any group of people is dehumanizing and immoral.

Practice: Analyzing a Definition Essay

1. Underline the thesis statement, and then restate it in your own words.

2. Why does the term *untouchable* require more than a one-sentence dictionary definition?

3. Where does Ajoy use examples to develop his definition? Where does he use narration?

4. Circle the transitional words and phrases that Ajoy uses to move readers through his definition. Does he need to add more transitions?

5. Summarize the essay's conclusion in your own words.

6. **T E S T** Ajoy's essay (see pages 119–20). Does he include all of the necessary elements?

7. What, specifically, did Ajoy change between his first and final drafts? Do you think all of his changes improved his essay? Is there anything else you would change?

13

Argumentation

13.1 Understanding Argumentation

Argumentative essays take a stand on a debatable issue — that is, an issue that has at least two sides (and can therefore be debated). An argument uses different kinds of *evidence* — facts, examples, and sometimes expert opinion — to persuade readers that a position has merit.

In addition to presenting your position, an argumentative essay should also address arguments against your position and *refute* them — that is, argue against them — by identifying factual errors or errors in logic. (If an opposing argument is particularly strong, you can concede its strength but go on to point out some weaknesses.) If you deal with opposing arguments in this way and your evidence is solid and your logic is sound, you will present a convincing argument.

13.2 Writing an Argumentative Essay

When you **TEST** your argumentative essay, make sure that it includes all the necessary elements (see page 40). Because argumentative essays often include outside sources, you should also review Chapters 17 and 18 in *Patterns for College Writing* to remind yourself how to integrate and document source material.

- **T** • **Thesis Statement** — The introduction of an argumentative essay should include a **thesis statement** that expresses the essay's main idea: the position you will take on the issue.

- **E** • **Evidence** — The body paragraphs should include supporting **evidence** — facts, examples, and expert opinion — to support the thesis statement convincingly. The topic sentence of each body paragraph should identify one point of support for your thesis. These points should be presented in **logical order**.

S • **Summary Statement** — The conclusion of an argumentative essay should include a strong **summary statement** that reinforces the essay's thesis — the position you take on the issue.

T • **Transitions** — An argumentative essay should include logical **transitional words and phrases** that show how your points are related and move readers through your argument.

13.3 Organizing an Argumentative Essay

An argumentative essay can be organized *inductively* or *deductively*. An **inductive argument** moves from the specific to the general — that is, from a group of specific observations to a general conclusion based on these observations. An inductive argument could begin by presenting facts, examples, and expert opinion about the benefits of investing in the stock market and end with the conclusion that people should be able to invest part of their Social Security contributions in the stock market.

A **deductive argument** moves from the general to the specific. A deductive argument begins with a **major premise** (a general statement that the writer believes his or her audience will accept) and then moves to a **minor premise** (a specific instance of the belief stated in the major premise). It ends with a **conclusion** that follows from the two premises. For example, an essay on physician-assisted suicide could be a deductive argument. It could begin with the major premise that all terminally ill patients who are in great pain should be given access to physician-assisted suicide. It could then go on to state and explain the minor premise that a particular patient is both terminally ill and in great pain, offering facts, examples, and the opinions of experts to support this premise. The essay could conclude that this patient should, therefore, be allowed the option of physician-assisted suicide. The deductive argument presented in the essay would have three parts.

MAJOR PREMISE	All terminally ill patients who are in great pain should be allowed to choose physician-assisted suicide.
MINOR PREMISE	John Lacca is a terminally ill patient who is in great pain.
CONCLUSION	Therefore, John Lacca should be allowed to choose physician-assisted suicide.

Before you present your argument, think about whether your readers are likely to be hostile toward, neutral toward, or in agreement with your position. Once you understand your audience, you can decide which points to make to support your argument. Try to achieve a balanced, moderate tone, and avoid name-calling or personal attacks.

Begin each paragraph of your argumentative essay with a topic sentence that clearly introduces a point in support of your thesis. Throughout your essay, include specific examples that will make your arguments persuasive. Keep in mind that arguments that rely on generalizations alone are not as convincing as those that include vivid details and specific examples.

In addition to presenting your case, your essay should also briefly summarize arguments *against* your position and **refute** them (that is, argue against them) by identifying factual errors or errors in logic. If an opposing argument is particularly strong, concede its strength—but try to point out some weaknesses as well. If you deal with opposing arguments in this way, your audience will see you as a fair and reasonable person.

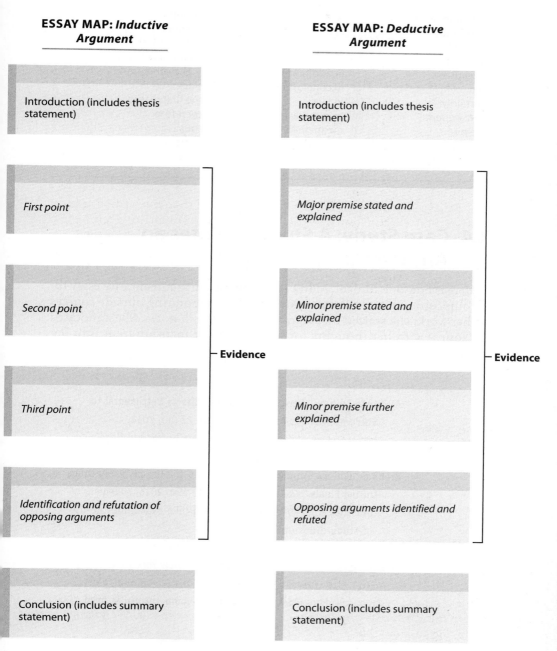

ESSAY MAP: *Inductive Argument*

Introduction (includes thesis statement)

First point

Second point

Third point

Identification and refutation of opposing arguments

⊢ **Evidence**

Conclusion (includes summary statement)

ESSAY MAP: *Deductive Argument*

Introduction (includes thesis statement)

Major premise stated and explained

Minor premise stated and explained

Minor premise further explained

Opposing arguments identified and refuted

⊢ **Evidence**

Conclusion (includes summary statement)

SOME TRANSITIONAL WORDS AND PHRASES FOR ARGUMENT

Transitions are important in argumentative essays. For example, transitional phrases such as *the first reason* and *another reason* tell readers they are moving from one point to another. In addition, the transitional phrases *one objection* and *another objection* indicate that a writer is addressing two opposing arguments.

accordingly	finally	nonetheless
admittedly	first . . . second . . .	of course
after all	for this reason	one . . . another
although	however	on the one hand . . . on
because	in addition	the other hand
but	in conclusion	since
certainly	in fact	the first reason
consequently	in summary	therefore
despite	meanwhile	thus
even so	moreover	to be sure
even though	nevertheless	truly

13.4 Case Study: A Student Writes an Argumentative Essay

Here is how one student, Marta Ramos, wrote an argumentative essay for her composition course. Because Marta was incorporating outside sources into her work, she started by organizing her research notes. She annotated each source with her thoughts for how she might incorporate it into her essay.

Works Cited

ADDitude Editors. "New Study: Adderall Effects Detrimental to
    Students Without ADHD." *ADDitude*, 23 Jul. 2018.
    https://www.additudemag.com/adderall-effects-college
    -students-without-adhd/.

Brennan, Collin. "Popping Pills: Examining the Use of 'Study Drugs'
    During Finals." *USA Today College*, 17 Mar. 2016, college
    .usatoday.com/2015/12/16/popping-pills-examining-the-use
    -of-study-drugs-during-fnals/.

    Good introduction to the topic. Could cite in overview section.

Cohen, Roger. "The Competition Drug." *The New York Times*, 4 Mar.
    2013, www.newyorktimes.com/2013/03/05/opinion/global
    /roger-cohen-adderall-the-academic-competition-drg.html.

Disturbing story about Steven Roderick. Could use a quotation from Roderick about his terrible experience.

Graf, William D., et al. "Pediatric Neuroenhancement: Ethical, Legal, Social, and Neurodevelopmental Implications." *Neurology*, vol. 80, no. 13, 26 Mar. 2013, pp. 1251–60. Scientific study on the effects of study drugs. Includes physical and side effects (that's the neurodevelopmental bit). Could use some of the legal stuff from here.

Krans, Brian. "Think Prescription Stimulants Like Adderall Improve Focus? They Don't." *Healthline*, 23 Aug. 2019, https://www .healthline.com/health-news/study-drug-dangers.

Oremus, Will. "The New Stimulus Package." *Slate*, 27 Mar. 2013, www .slate.com/articles/technology/superman/2013/03/adderall _ritalin_vyvanse_do_smart_pills_work_if_you_don_t_have _adhd.html. This article completely wrong. What a waste of my time.

Once she had her notes in order, Marta wrote down her thesis and used an informal outline to group her ideas.

Thesis: The risks of study drugs outweigh their advantages.
Background
    Research on Ritalin and Adderall
    Evidence
Negative effects
    Personality changes
    Instant gratification
Other problems
    No medical supervision
    Steven Roderick example
Argument to refute
    Like caffeine
    Adderall harmless

Using her informal outline as a guide, Marta wrote a draft of her essay. She focused on incorporating her sources, particularly in her refutation paragraph. She knew that in her second draft, she would need to make sure that she had used enough evidence, that she had correctly cited each source, and that she had not inadvertently committed plagiarism. Read through Marta's draft, and then answer the questions in the peer-editing worksheet on page 136.

Marta Ramos, First Draft

Say No

Many students routinely take prescription medications such as Ritalin or Adderall to improve their academic performance. On the one hand, students who take these medications say that they help them concentrate and improve their ability to study and to get high grades. On the other hand, medical professionals warn that the effects of prolonged exposure to these drugs can be harmful and, in some cases, even fatal. Unfortunately, these warnings have not stopped an increasing number of students from taking such drugs. They say that parental pressure and the need to succeed have forced them to take these extreme measures. Unfortunately, the risks that these drugs present far outweigh their supposed advantages.

Despite the claims of users, research published in the journal *Behavioural Brain Research* found that although people in study *felt* more focused, they "had no benefit to working memory" (Krans). Even worse, a 2018 study by researchers at Brown University and the University of Rhode Island showed that "the stimulant medication may actually impair working memory performance in college students without ADHD" (ADDitude Editors). Students often do not realize this, however, because researchers have concluded that Adderall, in particular, makes you think you're doing better than you actually are (Kranz). This probably accounts for why people are always talking about the drug's effectiveness. Students who take study drugs think they work, but there is little evidence to suggest they do.

Even though the physical effects of study drugs are obvious, there are other negative effects that can be subtle and quite insidious. Current research suggests that study drugs can change a person's personality completely. In other words, study drugs provide a false sense of self to students at a time when they should be testing their abilities and pursuing authenticity. It goes without saying that college is a time of important self-discovery for students and that any substance that interferes with this process is, therefore, harmful and should be avoided at all costs. Unfortunately, the temptation to take study drugs is encouraged by a society that values superficiality, instant gratification, and winning at all costs.

Another problem is that study drugs are often obtained illegally or under false pretenses. Students either buy them from friends or fake conditions such as Attention Deficit Disorder (ADD) to get doctors to prescribe them. Because Adderall is an amphetamine, its side effects are unpredictable — especially when it is abused or mixed with alcohol, a common practice for students celebrating after an exam. For this reason, taking drugs like Adderall without proper medical supervision can have severe physical and mental results. One student, Steven Roderick, cited in a *New York Times* article about study drugs, began taking Adderall during his first year in college. In the beginning, a small amount of the drug seemed to improve his academic performance, but as time went on, he needed to increase the dosage to get the same result. By his senior year, Roderick was taking large amounts of Adderall in the morning before classes and taking other drugs at night to get to sleep. Eventually, the Adderall stopped working, and because he couldn't concentrate, he was forced to drop out of college (Cohen).

Of course, not everyone agrees with this assessment of study drugs. Some argue that they are more like caffeinated drinks than other hard drugs such as steroids or amphetamines. In an article on Slate.com, Will Oremus asks, "What if Adderall turns out to be the new coffee — a ubiquitous, mostly harmless little helper that enables us to spend more time poring over spreadsheets and less time daydreaming or lolling about in bed?" The answer to this question is simple and straightforward. Unlike drinking coffee, the abuse of prescription drugs is not "mostly harmless." On the contrary, it can undermine the academic mission of colleges, it can damage the physical and mental well-being of students, and it can hurt society by compromising its core values.

Study drugs are dangerous and students need to be warned against them. Medical professionals should be on the lookout for students who are trying to fool them into prescribing Adderall. Parents should recognize the behavior associated with the excessive use of study drugs. Finally, colleges should make it clear to students that the use of study drugs is unacceptable and will not be tolerated. Only by adopting these measures can the use of study drugs finally be eliminated.

Works Cited

Cohen, Roger. "The Competition Drug." *The New York Times*,
    4 Mar. 2013, www.nytimes.com/2013/03/05/opinion/global
    /roger-cohen-adderall-the-academic-competition-drug.html?_r=0.
Krans, Brian. "Think Prescription Stimulants Like Adderall Improve
    Focus? They Don't." *Healthline*, 23 Aug. 2019, https://www
    .healthline.com/health-news/study-drug-dangers.

Oremus, Will. "The New Stimulus Package." *Slate*, 27 Mar. 2013,
www.slate.com/articles/technology/superman/2013/03
/adderall_ritalin_vyvanse_do_smart_pills_work_if_you_don_t
_have_adhd.html.

PEER-EDITING WORKSHEET: **ARGUMENTATION**

1. Does the essay take a stand on an issue? What is it? At what point does the writer state the thesis? Is the thesis debatable?

2. What evidence does the writer include to support the thesis? What additional evidence could the writer supply?

3. Has the writer used information from outside sources? If so, is documentation included? Identify any information the writer should have documented but did not.

4. Does the essay summarize and refute the opposing arguments? List these arguments.

5. How effective are the writer's refutations? Should the writer address any other arguments?

6. Does the essay use inductive reasoning? Deductive reasoning? Both? Provide an example of each type of reasoning used in the essay.

7. Does the writer use sources? Do they reinforce the writer's argument? Does the writer need to add additional sources?

8. Does the writer need to add a visual?

9. Does the essay include any logical fallacies? How would you correct these fallacies?

10. Do coordinating and subordinating conjunctions convey the logical and sequential connections between ideas?

11. How could the introduction be improved?

12. How could the conclusion be improved?

13.5 Analyzing an Argumentative Essay

When Marta finished her revisions, she prepared a final draft. Read her final draft, and then do the practice exercise that follows it.

Just Say No

Recently, the increase in the use of so-called study drugs has become a hotly debated subject. Many students now routinely take prescription medications such as Ritalin or Adderall to improve their academic performance (Brennan). On the one hand, students who take these medications say that they help them concentrate and improve their ability to study and to get high grades. On the other hand, medical professionals warn that the effects of prolonged exposure to these drugs can be harmful and in some cases even fatal. Unfortunately, these warnings have not stopped an ever-increasing number of students — both in high school and in college — from taking such drugs. They argue that parental pressure and the need to succeed have forced them to take extreme measures. In the final analysis, however, the risks that these drugs present far outweigh their supposed advantages.

Despite the claims of users, research published in the journal *Behavioural Brain Research* found that although people in study *felt* more focused, they "had no benefit to working memory" (Krans). Even worse, a 2018 study by researchers at Brown University and the University of Rhode Island showed that "the stimulant medication may actually impair working memory performance in college students without ADHD" (ADDitude Editors). Students often do not realize this, however, because researchers have concluded that Adderall, in particular, makes you think you're doing better than you actually are (Kranz). This probably accounts for the anecdotal evidence of the drug's effectiveness. In short, even though students who take study drugs think they work, there is little hard evidence to suggest they actually do.

Adding to the problem, study drugs are often obtained illegally or under false pretenses. Students either buy them from friends or fake conditions such as Attention Deficit Disorder (ADD) to get doctors to prescribe them. Because Adderall is an amphetamine, its side effects are unpredictable — especially when it is abused or mixed with alcohol. For this reason, taking drugs like Adderall without proper medical supervision can — and often does — have severe physical and mental consequences. For example, Steven Roderick, a student cited in a *New York Times* article about study drugs, began taking Adderall during his first year in college. In the beginning, a small amount of the drug seemed to improve his academic performance, but as time went on, he needed to increase the dosage to experience the same effect. By his senior year, Roderick was taking large amounts of Adderall in the morning before classes and taking other drugs at night to get to sleep. Eventually, the Adderall stopped working, and because he could not concentrate without it, he was forced to drop out of school (Cohen).

Even though the physical effects of study drugs are obvious, other negative effects can be subtle and quite insidious. Current research suggests that study drugs can "alter personality and constrain the very self that should be supported to live authentically" (Graf et al. 1257). In other words, study drugs provide a false sense of self to students at a time when they should be testing their abilities and pursuing authenticity. It goes without saying that college is a time of self-discovery and that any substance that interferes with this process is, therefore, harmful and should be avoided. Unfortunately, the temptation to take study drugs is encouraged by a society that values superficiality over depth, instant gratification over determination, and winning at all costs over fairness and personal development.

Of course, not everyone agrees with this assessment of study drugs. Some argue that concerns about these medications are overblown and that they are more like caffeinated drinks than steroids or amphetamines. In an article on Slate.com, Will Oremus asks, "What if Adderall turns out to be the new coffee — a ubiquitous, mostly harmless little helper that enables us to spend more time poring over spreadsheets and less time daydreaming or lolling about in bed?" The answer to this question is simple. Unlike drinking coffee, the abuse of illicitly obtained prescription drugs is not "mostly harmless." On the contrary, it can undermine the academic mission of colleges; it can damage the physical and mental well-being of students; and it can hurt society by compromising its core values.

Because of the dangers of study drugs, educators, medical professionals, and parents should inform students of the risks and discourage their use. Medical professionals should be on the lookout for students who are trying to fool them into prescribing Adderall. Parents should be educated to recognize the behavior associated with the excessive use of study drugs. Finally, colleges should make it clear to students that the use of study drugs is unacceptable and will not be tolerated. Only by adopting these measures can the use of study drugs be curtailed — and, eventually, eliminated.

Works Cited

ADDitude Editors. "New Study: Adderall Effects Detrimental to Students Without ADHD." *ADDitude*, 23 Jul. 2018. https://www.additudemag.com/adderall-effects-college-students-without-adhd/.

Brennan, Collin. "Popping Pills: Examining the Use of 'Study Drugs' during Finals." *USA Today College*, 16 Dec. 2015, college.usatoday.com/2015/12/16/popping-pills-examining-the-use-of-study-drugs-during-fnals/.

Cohen, Roger. "The Competition Drug." *The New York Times*, 4 Mar. 2013, www.nytimes.com/2013/03/05/opinion/global/roger-cohen-adderall-the-academic-competition-drug.html?_r=0.

Graf, William D., et al. "Pediatric Neuroenhancement: Ethical, Legal, Social, and Neurodevelopmental Implications." *Neurology*, vol. 80, no. 13, 26 Mar. 2013, pp. 1251–60.

Krans, Brian. "Think Prescription Stimulants Like Adderall Improve Focus? They Don't." *Healthline*, 23 Aug. 2019, https://www.healthline.com/health-news/study-drug-dangers.

Oremus, Will. "The New Stimulus Package." *Slate*, 27 Mar. 2013, www.slate.com/articles/technology/superman/2013/03/adderall_ritalin_vyvanse_do_smart_pills_work_if_you_don_t_have_adhd.html.

Practice: Analyzing an Argumentative Essay

1. What issue is Marta discussing? What is Marta's stance on that issue?

2. List the evidence Marta uses to support her thesis. Where does she include expert opinion?

3. Can you think of any other supporting evidence that Marta could have included? Should she have? Explain.

4. What opposing arguments does Marta mention?

5. How does Marta refute these arguments?

6. Circle the transitional words and phrases that Marta uses to move readers through her argument. Where, if anywhere, should more transitions be added?

7. **T E S T** Marta's essay (see pages 129–30). Does she include all the necessary elements?

8. Review the Guidelines for Preparing the Works-Cited List on page 744 of *Patterns for College Writing*. Does Marta's works-cited list follow all of these guidelines?

9. What, specifically, did Marta change between her first and final drafts? Do you think all of Marta's changes improved her essay? Explain.

PART THREE

Guide to Language and Mechanics

14

Grammatical Sentences

14.1 Fragments

A **fragment** is an incomplete sentence. In order to determine whether a sentence is complete or incomplete, you must first be able to identify the parts of a sentence.

Sentence Parts

A sentence always includes a subject (S) and a predicate (P). A sentence predicate is composed of a verb (V) and often includes its object (O) and a subject complement (SC).

The subject of a sentence identifies who or what the sentence is about. Often, the subject performs the action of the verb.

The predicate of a sentence includes a verb that expresses either an action or a state of being and tells something about the subject.

The object of a sentence identifies who or what receives the action described by the verb.

A subject complement completes the predicate by reiterating or describing the subject or object.

Fragments occur when a sentence is missing one of these parts: a subject, a verb/predicate, or both.

Fragment: Ingrid spent most of her day on the computer. *Tweeting and posting to Instagram.*

The second group of words is a fragment because it contains neither a subject nor a verb.

Complete: Ingrid spent most of her day on the computer, tweeting and posting to Instagram.

It is possible for a clause to contain both a subject and a verb and still be a fragment because it fails to express a complete thought.

Fragment: She refused to give up her social media time. *Even though she needed to do her homework.*

Notice how the second clause contains a subject (*she*) and a verb (*needed*) but fails to express a complete thought because of the subordinating conjunction *even though*.

Complete: Even though she needed to do her homework, she refused to give up her social media time.

Complete: She refused to give up her social media time even though she needed to do her homework.

Fragments as Phrases

A phrase is a small group of related words that may function as a part of speech *within a sentence* but cannot function as a complete sentence. There are two easy ways to fix fragments that are phrases: You can either link the phrase to a nearby sentence using punctuation, or you can add a subject and verb to the phrase and make it a complete sentence.

Fragment: We planned to go to Grandma's house. *Over the river and through the woods.*

Fragment: *Over the river and through the woods.*

Correct: We planned to go to Grandma's house, which is over the river and through the woods.

Correct: We drove over the river and through the woods.

Fragments as Subordinate Clauses

Unlike an independent clause, which contains a noun and a verb and expresses a complete thought, a subordinate clause — also known as a dependent clause — contains a noun and a verb but begins with a word (usually a subordinating conjunction) that does not allow the clause to stand on its own as a sentence. You may remove that conjunction to make the clause independent or combine the subordinate clause with an independent clause to make it a complete sentence.

Fragment: The car hit the tree. *When it went off the side of the road.*

Correct: The car hit the tree. It went off the side of the road.

Correct: The car hit the tree when it went off the side of the road.

Correct: When the car went off the side of the road, it hit the tree.

Notice that if the dependent clause with the subordinating conjunction introduces the main clause, you need a comma after the dependent clause. However, if the dependent clause follows the main clause, no comma is needed.

Fragments Containing Participles

A participle is a verb form that acts as an adjective by modifying a noun or noun phrase. It can also act as an adverb by modifying a verb or verb phrase. A participle alone can never function as the verb of a sentence. If a fragment contains a participle but no other verb, you must either change the participle to a main verb that describes the action or a state of being or link the fragment to a nearby sentence.

Fragment: *Howling* at the moon. The dog kept me awake all night.

Correct: The dog howled at the moon. It kept me awake all night.

Correct: Howling at the moon, the dog kept me awake all night.

Fragments in Compound Predicates

A compound predicate tells more than one thing about the subject of a sentence by using two verbs joined by a conjunction. The second verb in a compound predicate must be in the same sentence as its subject.

Fragment: Lita can speak English and Spanish. *And write in both too.*

Correct: Lita can speak and write in Spanish and English.

14.2 Comma Splices and Fused Sentences

A comma splice occurs when two independent clauses are joined only by a comma. An independent clause is one that can stand alone as a complete sentence.

Comma Splice: The day was hot, the night was even hotter.

Correct: The day was hot. The night was even hotter.

A fused sentence occurs when two independent clauses are joined with no conjunction or proper punctuation.

Fused: The day was hot the night was even hotter.

Correct: The day was hot, but the night was even hotter.

Using a Period to Fix a Comma Splice or Fused Sentence

One way to correct a comma splice or fused sentence is to separate each of the independent clauses by placing a period between them. Each clause becomes its own stand-alone sentence.

Comma Splice: The comma splice is easy to identify, it uses a comma instead of a period or semicolon to separate two independent clauses.

Correct: The comma splice is easy to identify. It uses a comma instead of a period or semicolon to separate two independent clauses.

Using a Comma and Coordinating Conjunction to Fix a Comma Splice or Fused Sentence

Another way to correct a comma splice or fused sentence is to connect each clause with a coordinating conjunction, such as *and, nor, or, but, yet,* or *so.* A coordinating conjunction often signals the relationship between the two clauses in a fused or spliced sentence. In the example below, using the coordinating conjunction *but* indicates the clauses are in some way opposite from each other. When you use a conjunction to correct a fused sentence, always place a comma before the conjunction.

Comma Splice: T.J. is an excellent basketball player, he will not enter the draft this season.

Correct: T.J. is an excellent basketball player, but he will not enter the draft this season.

Using a Semicolon to Fix a Comma Splice or Fused Sentence

You may correct a comma splice or fused sentence by using a semicolon. Using a semicolon rather than a period between two clauses in a fused or spliced sentence emphasizes the relationship between the ideas in each clause. The effect is often that both clauses appear equally important. Do not capitalize the first word of the second independent clause.

Comma Splice: Ellen joined the track team, she's a great runner.

Correct: Ellen joined the track team; she's a great runner.

Fixing a Comma Splice or Fused Sentence with a Subordinating Conjunction

Sometimes one independent clause in a fused sentence is more important than the other. In such cases, you may want to use a subordinating conjunction, such as *after, before,* or *unless* to fix the sentence. Subordinating the less important clause places emphasis on the more relevant part of the sentence. As with the semicolon, this strategy allows you to illustrate how ideas relate to each other in a sentence.

Fused: Alex always gets speeding tickets he will probably lose his license.

Correct: Because Alex always gets speeding tickets, he will probably lose his license.

Using a Conjunctive Adverb and Semicolon to Fix a Comma Splice or Fused Sentence

A conjunctive adverb explains the relationship between two independent clauses. Such relationships may include time (*afterward, earlier*), opposition (*conversely, on the other hand*), likeness (*similarly, accordingly*), or summary (*as a result, thus*). Conjunctive adverbs can be used to correct comma splices or fused sentences; to make this correction, place a semicolon before the conjunctive adverb and a comma afterward, as in the example below.

Comma Splice: Hardly anyone at the wedding reception left early, the guests stayed and danced until four in the morning.

Correct: Hardly anyone at the wedding reception left early; on the contrary, guests stayed and danced until four in the morning.

14.3 Verbs

Action verbs get their name from their function: they describe action (*ran, jumped*). Action verbs are what you normally think of when you think of verbs. Linking verbs join the subject of a sentence to its complement (a word or phrase that describes the subject) either by depicting a state of being (*be, appear, seem, sound*) or a result of some kind (*become, get*). Helping or auxiliary verbs (*can, may, will*) are the least common verbs and always precede the main verb in a sentence, thus clarifying its action.

Linking Verbs

A linking verb (LV) illustrates the relationship between the sentence subject (S) and the subject complement (SC), which can be a noun, a pronoun, or an adjective.

Esperanza (S) *was* (LV) this year's *homecoming queen* (SC). [SC is a noun]

The *basketball* (S) *is* (LV) *his* (SC). [SC is a pronoun]

The puppy's *fur* (S) *feels* (LV) *soft* (SC) and *silky* (SC). [SCs are adjectives]

Verbs that function as linking verbs may sometimes function as transitive verbs, depending on context. Transitive verbs take one or more objects.

The air *felt* very cold [Linking verb *felt* + subject complement *cold*]

I *felt* the wall to find my way in the dark. [Transitive verb *felt* + direct object *wall*]

Helping Verbs

A helping verb affects the tense of the verb it accompanies and indicates shades of meaning in the sentence. The combination of a helping verb and a main verb is known as a verb phrase. Although the parts of a verb phrase often appear side by side in a sentence, other words may sometimes separate them.

In a few moments, Beyoncé *is going* to walk onstage.

I *have told* you many times that the essay is due at the end of the semester.

Samira *will* not *ask* her mother to drive us home from band practice today.

Principal Parts of Verbs

The principal parts of a verb are the different forms it can take. Verbs have three principal parts: the infinitive (or base), the past tense, and the past participle.

The infinitive is the simplest form of a verb and is generally preceded by the word *to* (*to decide, to open, to work*). Infinitives alone can never serve as the main verb in a sentence.

The past tense verb indicates an action completed in the past (*decided, opened, worked*).

The past participle is always combined with a helping verb and depicts action at various times, both future and past (*have decided, has opened, will have worked*). When the helping verb is a form of *be*, it creates the passive voice. In passive voice sentences, the subject of the sentence receives the action of the verb.

Verbs also have a present participle, formed by adding *-ing* to the infinitive (*deciding, opening, working*). Present participles have multiple uses, including forming the present progressive tense (I am *deciding*), modifying a noun or pronoun (the *lying* scoundrel), or serving as gerunds, which function as nouns in a sentence (*Writing* is his passion). Like infinitives, present participles can never serve as the main verb of a sentence.

Forming the Past Tense and Past Participle of Regular and Irregular Verbs

To form the past tense of a regular verb, add *-d* or *-ed* to the infinitive. Regular verbs with infinitives that end in *-e* take *-d* in the past tense; verbs that don't end in *-e* take *-ed*.

Infinitive: to jump

Past Tense: jumped

Past Participle: jumped

Although most verbs are regular verbs, numerous irregular verbs do not end in *-d* or *-ed* in the past tense (*dug, slept, chose, hurt*). Like regular verbs, their principal parts include the present, the past, and the past participle.

Verb Tenses

A verb's tense indicates the time of its action or state of being. The three simple tenses are present, past, and future.

The perfect tenses describe actions or events that occurred in the past but are linked to a later time, often the present.

The progressive tenses indicate actions or conditions continuing in the past, present, or future.

Simple Tenses

Present: I speak, I dance

Past: I spoke, I danced

Future: I will speak, I will dance

Perfect Tenses

Present perfect: I have spoken, I have danced

Past perfect: I had spoken, I had danced

Future perfect: I will have spoken, I will have danced

Progressive Tenses

Present progressive: I am speaking, I am dancing

Past progressive: I was speaking, I was dancing

Future progressive: I will be speaking, I will be dancing

Forming the Simple Present Tense

The simple present tense typically indicates actions that take place once, repeatedly, or continuously in the present. The simple present form of a regular verb is based on the infinitive form. For the third person singular, add -s or -es to the infinitive.

	Singular	*Plural*
First Person:	I wonder	we wonder
Second Person:	you wonder	you (all) wonder
Third Person:	he/she/it wonders they wonder	they wonder

Most irregular verbs also take the same form as regular verbs in the simple present.

To choose

I choose, you/they choose, he/she/it chooses

we choose, you (all) choose, they choose

However, some irregular verbs do not add -s or -es to the infinitive to form the simple present.

To have

I have, you/they have, he/she/it has

As noted above, the simple present tense can describe an action happening currently.

I *choose* to do my homework.

However, it may also be used to describe a future action.

I *will choose* to do my homework.

When using the simple present to describe a future action, it's often helpful to contextualize with words like *before*, *after*, or *when*.

Before I choose to do my homework, I will check my email.

Forming the Simple Past Tense

The simple past tense is used to indicate actions that have already finished.

I *groomed* my horse yesterday. [Regular verb]

I *rode* my horse yesterday. [Irregular verb]

You may also use the helping verb *did* alongside the infinitive form of the main verb in a sentence to emphasize a past action or ask a question about an action performed in the past.

I rode.

I did ride. [Emphasizes the action]

Why did I ride? [Asks a question]

Forming the Simple Future Tense

The simple future tense is used to depict actions that are expected to happen but haven't yet. It is formed by adding *will* to the infinitive form of the verb.

	Singular	*Plural*
First Person:	I will read	we will read
Second Person:	you will read	you (all) will read
Third Person:	he/she/it will read they will read	they will read

Forming the Perfect Tenses

Perfect tenses are used to depict actions completed at the time of another action. They are formed by adding a form of the helping verb *have* to the past participle (for example, *acted, chosen*) of the main verb. The tense of *have* determines the tense of the entire verb phrase.

The present perfect tense indicates actions that were completed at any point prior to the present, and its helping verb is in the present tense (*have* or *has*).

Uncontrolled logging *has destroyed* many tropical forests.

The present perfect can also show an action completed before another action happening in the present ("I *have decided* that I want to audition for the school play") or an action beginning in the past and continuing into the present.

Ms. Green *has been* teaching for thirty years.

We *have been* rehearsing since the first week of school.

The past perfect tense indicates actions that were completed before another action that also took place in the past. Its helping verb is in the past tense (*had*).

Homesteaders found that speculators *had* already *taken* all of the good land.

The future perfect tense indicates actions that will be completed by or before a point in the future. Its helping verb is in the future tense (*will have*).

In ten years, our investment *will have* doubled.

After today's trip to the library, *will* you *have studied* enough to get an A on the final exam?

Forming Simple Progressive Tenses

Progressive tenses indicate that an action is continuing or in progress. They are created by combining a form of the helping verb *be* with the present participle of the main verb (for example, *playing, running*). The tense of *be* determines the tense of the entire verb phrase.

The present progressive tense indicates actions that are ongoing or continuing into the present time. Its helping verb is in the present tense (*am, is, are*).

Yolanda *is applying* for a scholarship.

The present progressive of *go* can also be used to depict a future action when it is used in a context (typically with an infinitive phrase) that makes the time clear.

Carrie *is going to help* me with my essay after school. [*to help* = infinitive phrase]

The past progressive tense indicates continuous actions that took place in the past, often (but not always) with specified limits. Its helping verb is in the past tense (*was, were*).

In the 1980s, many baby boomers *were becoming* parents.

I *was cleaning* my room when you texted me.

The future progressive tense indicates actions that will take place continuously in the future. Its helping verb is in the future tense (*will be*).

The team *will be competing* in the NCAA tournament this year.

Forming Perfect Progressive Tenses

The perfect progressive tense depicts continuing actions that began in the past.

The present perfect progressive tense indicates an action that began in the past and continues to occur in the present. It is formed by adding the present perfect of the helping verb *to be* (*has been, have been*) to the present participle (for example, *running, playing*) of the main verb.

The two sides *have been trying* to settle the case out of court.

The past perfect progressive tense indicates a continuing action that ended before another past action. It is formed by adding the past perfect form of the helping verb *be* (*had been*) to the present participle of the main verb.

Carter *had been planning* a naval career before his father died.

The future perfect progressive tense indicates an action that will continue into the future and be completed before or continue beyond another future action. It is formed by adding *will have been* to the present participle of the main verb.

By next July, I *will have been living* in Tucson for eight years.

Verb Voice

Voice is the feature of transitive verbs that tells whether the subject of a sentence is acting or being acted upon.

Active voice indicates that the subject is acting. Principal parts and helping verbs make up the active voice.

The detective questioned him.

Passive voice indicates that the subject is being acted upon. To construct a verb phrase in the passive voice, add a form of *be* to a past participle.

He was questioned by the detective.

It's generally preferable to use the active voice in academic writing because it makes the prose more immediate and clearly indicates who is doing what. Because the passive voice de-emphasizes sentence subjects, it can make prose vague and more difficult to understand.

Verb Mood

The mood of the verb indicates the purpose and intent of the sentence. In other words, verb mood indicates whether the writer or speaker is stating a fact, giving a command, or describing something that is either conditional (maybe true) or contrary to fact (untrue).

Indicative Mood

Most verbs are in the indicative mood, which is used to state a fact, ask a question, or express an opinion.

The geese landed on the field in a flock.

Where are you going?

People should recycle their garbage.

Imperative Mood

The imperative mood is used to make a request or give a command or direction. The subject of an imperative sentence is always *you*, but it is generally omitted from the sentence. Verbs in imperative sentences always take the infinitive, or base, form.

Please *buy* today's newspaper on your way home. [*You* please buy . . .]

Sit down right now! [*You* sit down right now!]

Use the socket wrench to loosen the lug nuts on the tire. [*You* use the socket wrench . . .]

Subjunctive Mood

The subjunctive mood is used to explore a hypothetical situation or express a wish, requirement, suggestion, or condition contrary to fact.

If a clause opens with *that* and expresses a requirement, it is in the subjunctive mood and its verb should be in the infinitive form.

It is our policy that volunteers *contribute* fifteen hours a week.

When the subjunctive mood describes a hypothetical situation or a condition that is wishful, doubtful, or outright contrary to fact, it is often found in a clause that begins with the word *if*. It may also follow a verb that expresses doubt. The verb *to be* becomes *were* in the subjunctive mood. All other verbs take the simple past tense in the subjunctive mood.

I wish I *were* in Hawaii right now.

If the government *prohibited* the sale of tobacco nationwide, the cancer mortality rate would decline.

However, when an event, action, or condition was contrary to fact at some point in the past, use the past perfect tense instead of the simple past to form the subjunctive mood.

If I *had been* in the game instead of on the sidelines, we *would have* won.

14.4 Subject-Verb Agreement

A sentence's subject and verb must agree in number. If the subject of the verb is singular, the verb form must be singular; if the subject of the verb is plural, the verb form must be plural.

The *athletes* (S) *were* (V) the first group to finish their assignment.

To make a present tense verb singular, you must add an "s." Plural verbs have no "s."

My *puppy* (S) *barks* (V) all night.

My *puppies* (S) **bark** (V) all night.

Interrupting Words or Phrases

A verb must agree in number (singular or plural) with its subject, regardless of whether other words come between the subject and the verb.

The *cars* (S), two Fords, a Lincoln, and a Nissan, *were* (V) for sale in the lot down the street.

The *bride* (S), along with her bridesmaids, *was* (V) late to the wedding.

A verb must also agree with its subject, even when the subject follows the verb.

Where *was* (V) your *brother* (S) when you got home?

Inside the cabinet *were* (V) the *tools* (S) he needed to fix the chair.

The subject and verb(s) in a sentence must agree in person, or the point of view being expressed. First person describes one's own perspective (*I am, we are*). Second person describes someone being addressed (*you are*). Third person describes others' perspectives (*he is, she is, it is, they are*).

I (S) *was* (V) the only person at home last night.

They (S) *were* (V) eager for spring break to arrive.

Titles That Are Subjects

When a subject of the sentence is a title of a book, movie, play, or work of art, it calls for a singular verb.

The Reivers (S), published in 1962, *is* (V) the last novel written by William Faulkner.

Singular Nouns That End in *-s*

Singular nouns that end in *-s* take singular verbs.

The *bus was* crowded this morning.

Statistics was my worst subject in school.

Subjects Joined by *and*

Subjects joined by *and* usually take a plural verb.

The cat and the dog *play* well together.

However, when *each* or *every* is used to specify that two singular subjects are separate actors in a sentence, the verb must be singular.

Each dog and cat in the shelter *is* well cared for.

Every dog and cat in the shelter *is* available for adoption.

Subjects Joined by *or* or *nor*

When a sentence contains two subjects that are joined by *or* or *nor*, the verb should agree with the subject that is closer to the verb.

Either the dog or the kittens *are* available for adoption.

Neither the kittens nor the dog *is* available for adoption.

Collective Nouns

Most collective nouns (for example, *group, committee, audience*) take singular verbs.

The team wearing red and black uniforms *controls* the ball.

When members of a group act as individuals, the accompanying verb should be plural.

Usually, the team wearing red and black uniforms *scatter* in all directions when the game is over.

Indefinite Pronouns

Indefinite pronouns are pronouns that do not refer to specific persons or things.

Some indefinite pronouns (*another, anybody, anyone, anything, each, either, everybody, everyone, everything, much, neither, nobody, no one, nothing, one, other, somebody, someone, something*) take singular verbs.

Each of the plays *depicts* a hero undone by a tragic flaw.

Other indefinite pronouns (*all, any, enough, more, most, none, some*) use either a singular or plural verb depending on their meaning.

All of the cake *was eaten.* [*All* refers to *cake*]

All of the candidates *promise* to improve schools. [*All* refers to *candidates*]

Subordinate Clauses with a Relative Pronoun as the Subject

When the subject of a subordinate clause is a relative pronoun (*who, which, that*), the verb should agree with that pronoun's antecedent — the word to which the relative pronoun refers.

Guilt, jealousy, and fear are ingredients *that go* into creating stereotypes. [The antecedent of *that* is the third person noun *ingredients*. Therefore, the verb in the subordinate clause *go* is in the third person plural form.]

Linking Verbs

When a linking verb connects two nouns, the first noun is the subject of the sentence and the second noun is the subject complement. The linking verb should agree with the subject, not the subject complement.

Nero Wolfe's passion was orchids. [*Nero Wolfe* is the subject; *orchids* is the subject complement. The verb *was* agrees with the subject.]

14.5 Pronoun Reference

Pronouns often refer to a noun, noun phrase, noun clause, or pronoun that was named or implied previously. The word, phrase, or clause the pronoun refers back to is called the antecedent; often, the antecedent is the subject or object of the clause in which the pronoun appears.

Tom invested all of *his* money in building a time machine. [*Tom* is the antecedent of *his*; using the pronoun is better than writing *Tom invested all of Tom's money in building a time machine.*]

At times, the antecedent may appear in a different clause or even a different sentence from the pronoun. There can be multiple antecedents in a sentence or passage.

Because *Tom* wanted to build a *time machine, he* invested all of *his* money in *it*. [*Tom* is the antecedent of *he* and *his*. *Time machine* is the antecedent of *it*.]

Both pronouns and nouns can be antecedents.

Even though some *people* thought *it* was a foolish idea, *they* also invested money in his *time machine*. [The noun *people* in the first clause is the antecedent of the pronoun *they* in the second clause. The noun phrase *time machine* in the second clause refers back to the pronoun *it* in the first clause.]

Naming a Pronoun's Antecedent

It is important to clearly identify the antecedent of each pronoun; otherwise, your writing may confuse readers. This is especially true for pronouns such as *it*, *this*, *that*, and *which*.

Unclear: She read a review of the book that confused her. [Was it the book or the review that confused her?]

Clear: She read a review of the book, a work that confused her. [Now it is clear that it was the book that confused her.]

Possessive nouns, such as *Tom's*, *José's*, and *cat's*, cannot work as antecedents.

Incorrect: In Juanita's story, she described spending the night in a haunted house. (This is confusing because *she* refers to Juanita, not the story.)

Correct: In her story, Juanita described spending the night in a haunted house. [Now, the connection between *her* and *Juanita* is clear.]

Adjective Clauses and Relative Pronouns

An adjective clause usually begins with a relative pronoun, such as *who*, *which*, or *that*. These relative pronouns clarify the relationship between an independent clause and an adjective clause. Use *who* to refer to people and *which* to refer to things. *That* can refer to both people and things, depending on context. Use *that* to introduce an adjective clause when it defines or specifies necessary information about the independent clause. Use *which* to introduce additional, but not necessary, information about the independent clause.

The Boone River, *which* flows intermittently during most of the year, overflowed after the storm. [The clause *which flows intermittently during most of the year* offers additional information that is interesting, but not necessary, about the river. Note that the clause is set off by commas.]

The river *that* overflowed last week does not generally reach flood levels. [The clause *that overflowed last week* provides information that specifies which river is referred to; therefore, it is necessary to the meaning of the sentence. Note that the clause is not set off by commas.]

In formal writing, a relative pronoun should be included when it is the subject within an adjective clause.

The Girl with the Dragon Tattoo is a book *that* gained a great deal of critical acclaim.

In informal writing or speaking, relative pronouns are commonly omitted when they are understood as an implied part of the sentence. Although this is common usage, it is generally best to avoid dropping the relative pronoun in formal writing.

Informal: *The Girl with the Dragon Tattoo* is one book I'd like to read.

Formal: *The Girl with the Dragon Tattoo* is one book *that* I'd like to read.

Informal: Here is a vase you can display the flowers in.

Formal: Here is a vase *in which* to display the flowers.

Informal: There is the man we think robbed the bank.

Formal: There is the man *who* we think robbed the bank.

There are two additional relative pronouns that also begin adjective clauses: *whose* (the possessive form of *who*) and *whom* (the object form of *who*).

Whose begins an adjective clause that describes something that belongs to or is a part of someone or something mentioned in the independent clause.

This tiny hummingbird, whose wings have been known to beat as many as eighty beats per second, is called the amethyst woodstar.

Whom stands in for the noun that receives the action of the verb in an adjective clause.

Formal: Bradley Cooper was the actor whom I met when I was in Hollywood. [*Bradley Cooper* is the subject of the main clause; *whom* is the object of the verb *met* in the relative clause and refers to *Bradley Cooper.*]

Informal: Bradley Cooper was the actor I met when I was in Hollywood. [*Whom* is understood as the object of the verb *met.*]

Whose is the only possessive relative pronoun; it is used to refer to persons, animals, and things. It takes the place of a possessive pronoun and must be followed by a noun. Using *who's* (the contraction for *who is* and *who has*) instead of the relative pronoun *whose* is a relatively common mistake.

Incorrect: The man who's car was stolen also lost his wallet with $500 in it.

Correct: The man whose car was stolen also lost his wallet with $500 in it.

14.6 Pronoun-Antecedent Agreement

Person, Number, and Gender

A pronoun must always agree with its antecedent in person (first, second, third), number (singular, plural), and gender (masculine, feminine, ungendered, or nonbinary). Please be aware, however, that although the pronouns *they* and *there* have historically been considered plural pronouns, they are often used as singular personal pronouns as well. If possible, try to confirm the preferred pronouns of someone about whom you are writing.

Incorrect: At tonight's meeting, please ask the *board* for *her* opinions on the matter. [*Board* is plural; *her* is singular.]

Correct: At tonight's meeting, please ask the *board* for *their* opinions on the matter.

Incorrect: *Each* of the students was prepared with *his* homework. [This assumes that the writer knows that the entire class is made up of boys; if the class includes people who do not identify as male, the writer's choice can be considered sexist]

Correct: *All* of the students were prepared with *their* homework. [Changing *each* (singular) to *all* (plural) resolves the error.]

While some authors may use *his or her* with *each* (singular), that is not recommended because it is not a fully inclusive option.

Antecedents Joined by *and*

When two or more words joined by *and* function as the subject of the sentence, they form a plural, compound subject. A compound subject, when functioning as an antecedent, requires a plural pronoun.

Millie, Isaac, and Ralph focused their attention on *their* tests.

However, if the nouns in a compound subject refer to the same person, the antecedent is singular and the pronoun that refers to it is also singular.

The *producer and star* of the movie always eats *her* breakfast before going on set.

Antecedents Joined by *or* or *nor*

When an antecedent is a compound subject joined by *or* or *nor*, its pronoun must agree with the word that is closer to it.

Neither *Isaac nor the girls* brought *their* uniforms to school.

Singular Indefinite Pronoun Antecedents

When an antecedent is a singular indefinite pronoun (*another, any, anybody, anyone, anything, each, either, everybody, everyone, everything, much, neither, nobody, no one, nothing, one, other, somebody, someone, something*), it takes a singular pronoun.

One of the homesteaders abandoned *his* land.

Collective Noun Antecedents

Collective nouns generally refer to a group acting as a unit (for example, *chorus, team, staff*). Most collective nouns used as antecedents take singular pronouns.

The *committee* was dedicated to meeting *its* goals.

If group members in a collective noun act as individuals, the noun takes a plural pronoun instead.

Because the *committee* couldn't agree, *their* meeting was a disaster.

14.7 Adjectives and Adverbs

Adjectives are words that describe a person, an object, a place, or an idea embodied in a noun, noun phrase, noun clause, or pronoun. Generally, an adjective comes before the word or words it describes. However, this is not the case when an adjective follows either a form of the verb *to be* or a verb that refers to appearance or the senses (*seem, appear, feel, taste, smell, sound*).

The *old* man wore a *green* sweater, *torn* pants, and a *dirty* overcoat.

The jam tart tasted *delicious*.

Adverbs are words that describe verbs, adjectives, or other adverbs in terms of time (*frequently*, *rarely*), place (*here*, *there*), and manner (*quickly*, *slowly*). Adverbs are frequently formed by adding -*ly* to adjectives. When adverbs describe verbs, they often immediately precede or follow the verb, but sometimes they may be separated from the verb.

The team left the field *silently*.

When an adverb describes an adjective, it places greater emphasis on the adjective.

The dog who attacked that child is *really* vicious and should be put down.

When an adverb describes another adverb, it places greater emphasis on the second adverb.

She played the piano concerto *very rapidly*.

Sometimes the same word (for example, *fast*, *late*, *hard*) can be either an adjective or an adverb, depending on its function in the sentence.

The patient *arrived late* for surgery. [*Late* describes the verb, *arrived*; therefore, it is an adverb.]

The *patient* was *late*. [*Late* describes the *patient*; therefore, it is an adjective.]

Adjectives as Subject and Object Complements

An adjective may be used as a subject complement or object complement. A subject complement is a word or phrase (commonly an *adjective phrase*, *noun phrase*, or *pronoun*) that follows a linking verb and describes or renames the subject of a sentence. An object complement is a word or phrase that follows a direct object, renaming, describing, or locating it.

The abandoned farmhouse *looked ready to fall down*. [The adjective phrase *looked ready to fall down* describes the *farmhouse*.]

Good and *Well*, *Real* and *Really*

Good is always an adjective and *well* is the corresponding adverb.

Incorrect: She plays the piano *good* enough to be a star.

Correct: She plays the piano *well* enough to be a star.

Real is always an adjective and *really* is always an adverb.

Incorrect: Even though he played the trumpet *good*, he was *real* disappointed in his performance.

Correct: Even though he played the trumpet *well*, he was *really* disappointed in his performance.

Forming Comparatives and Superlatives with Most Adjectives and Adverbs

In addition to their simple forms, adjectives and adverbs have two other forms: comparative and superlative, both of which are used to make comparisons. In comparing two things, we want to identify which one is the greater; in comparing more than two things, we want to identify which one is the greatest. The key to comparatives is in the previous sentence. We use the term *comparative* to distinguish which of two things is better; the term *superlative* distinguishes between three or more things.

Form the comparative of most adjectives by adding *-er* to the word and the superlative by adding *-est* to the word.

> Rondae Hollis-Jefferson was the *taller* of the two basketball players who were interviewed, but he was not the *tallest* on the team.

The comparative and superlative of many adjectives with multiple syllables are formed by placing *more* and *most* before the adjective rather than *-er* and *-est* at the end of the word.

> Robert Downey Jr.'s performance was the *most powerful* of his career.

Comparative and superlative forms of many adverbs are formed by placing *more* and *most* before the adverb. However, short adverbs that end in *-ly* usually take *-er* and *-est* in the comparative and superlative.

> Enrique built his model airplane *more carefully* than Jonathan.

> Jamal arrived *earlier* than the other applicants.

Use the comparative *less* and the superlative *least* to construct negative comparisons.

> Students are committing errors with adverbs *less frequently* than they did a week ago.

> Among the members of the JV soccer team, Hugo was the *least ready* to join varsity.

Adjectives and Adverbs That Are Already Comparative or Superlative

Some adjectives and adverbs, such as *more* and *most*, already suggest comparatives and superlatives. Therefore, the words *more* and *most* should be omitted in sentences with adjectives and adverbs (*good, better, best*) that are already comparative and superlative.

> **Incorrect:** Antoine and Michael are both excellent soccer players, but Antoine is *more better*.

> **Correct:** Antoine and Michael are both excellent soccer players, but Antoine is *better*.

14.8 Shifts

A shift is a syntactical change—that is, a change in wording that allows a writer to portray various points of view or points in time. However, unnecessary shifts can lead to reader confusion.

Shifts in Verb Tense

Verb tenses should remain consistent throughout a piece of writing unless the time changes.

Inconsistent: Some people never really *settle* into a profession; these people only *took* jobs when they *needed* food or shelter.

Consistent: Some people never really *settle* into a profession; these people only *take* jobs when they *need* food and shelter.

If the time described in a passage of writing changes, the verb tense must also change with it. Even though there are several tense shifts in the example below, they clearly and succinctly delineate each time change.

I don't like my science class this year. I am having a hard time keeping up with the lessons. Last year, I did much better. I scored A's on all my tests, and all the work was easy to complete. I don't know why I'm struggling this year. I will ask my teacher for help. She is always available and willing to work with a struggling student.

When writing about literature, use the present tense to describe action happening within the book. However, you may use any applicable tense when discussing the work itself.

In *Gone with the Wind*, Scarlett is so obsessed with Ashley Wilkes that she cannot see how much he actually loves Melanie.

Margaret Mitchell first published *Gone with the Wind* in 1936.

Shifts in Verb Voice

Verb voice should remain consistent in writing. If you are using the active voice, do not switch to the passive voice, or vice versa.

Inconsistent: My *grandmother was* a wise woman, but her *wisdom was ignored* by most of the family.

Consistent: My *grandmother was* a wise woman, but most of the *family ignored* her wisdom.

Shifts in Person

Person refers to the relationship between a sentence's subject and its verb. It indicates whether the subject is speaking about itself (first person *I* or *we*), being spoken to (second person *you*), or being spoken about (third person *he, she, they, it*).

First person (*I, we*) helps establish a personal, informal relationship with readers. Novelists and short-story authors use first person when they want their readers to identify and empathize with the narrator. Second person (*you*) creates an immediacy that places a reader within the narrative and makes the reader feel like an active participant in the story. Third person (*he, she, they, it*) allows a writer to portray multiple points of view.

Person should remain consistent and appropriate to the content and the writer's purpose throughout a passage of writing.

Inconsistent: If *you* eat sensibly and watch *your* caloric intake, most *people* should be able to maintain *their* desired weight. (This also represents a *shift in number*, from a single person to more than one person.)

Consistent: If *you* eat sensibly and watch *your* caloric intake, *you* should be able to maintain *your* desired weight.

For the most part, avoid use of second person *you* in academic writing. It is too vague and can unintentionally offend your audience. Always strive to identify the specific group to which you are referring.

Incorrect: When you are released from prison, adjusting to the outside world can be hard. [If you are addressing a professor who takes pride in never even receiving a parking ticket, this might not go over very well.]

Correct: When inmates are released from prison, they often struggle to adjust to the outside world.

Shifts in Mood

A verb's mood indicates the writer's attitude toward a particular topic, and it should remain consistent. Most mood shifts are from indicative to imperative.

Inconsistent: *Bend your knees,* and you *should keep your eyes on the ball.* [The mood shifts from the indicative to the imperative.]

Consistent: *Bend your knees,* and *keep your eye on the ball.* [This sentence is entirely in the imperative.]

Effective Sentences

15.1 Misplaced and Dangling Modifiers

Words, phrases, and clauses that describe other words in a sentence are called modifiers. They modify the meaning of the words they describe by adding detail or specificity.

Misplaced Modifiers

The position of a modifier within a sentence is important. If a modifier is placed too far away from the word it describes, the sentence may become confusing or unclear. When a modifier's placement does not clearly indicate which word it describes, it is called a misplaced modifier.

Misplaced modifiers can be fixed by moving modifiers closer to the words they describe.

Misplaced: The dancers discussed techniques for doing complicated leaps and turns *in the car*.

The placement of this modifier suggests that the discussion was about *leaps and turns in the car*, but logic suggests that *in the car* describes where the discussion occurred, rather than the leaps and turns.

Therefore, the modifier should be placed nearer to the verb *discussed*:

Revised: *In the car*, the dancers discussed techniques for doing complicated leaps and turns.

Squinting Modifiers

In some sentences, a modifier can cause confusion even when it is adjacent to the word or phrase it describes. A squinting modifier is a modifier that could potentially describe either the word that precedes it or the word that follows. To fix a squinting modifier, adjust the placement or revise the sentence so that the modifier clearly modifies only one word or phrase.

Squinting: When learning a foreign language, practicing *frequently* improves confidence and fluency.

In the preceding sentence, it is unclear whether *frequently* modifies *practicing* or *improves*. If we assume that *frequently* is meant to modify *practicing*, the revised sentence could look like this:

> **Revised:** When learning a foreign language, frequently practicing improves confidence and fluency.

> **Revised:** When learning a foreign language, frequent practice improves confidence and fluency.

Dangling Modifiers

When a modifier describes an action or a state of being, the doer of that action or noun experiencing that state of being must be clearly named; otherwise, the modifier dangles from the sentence like a loose thread.

> **Dangling:** Exhausted from a long night of studying, the test seemed to go on forever.

> **Dangling:** After eating five tacos, a nap sounded like a good idea to Mark.

In the first sentence above, the modifier *exhausted from a long night of studying* cannot describe the only noun in the main clause: *the test*. A person can be exhausted from a long night of studying, but a test cannot. In the second sentence, the placement of the noun *nap* implies that the five tacos were eaten, not by Mark, but by a *nap*. To fix these dangling modifiers, first determine what noun or pronoun the dangler is supposed to modify. Then, add it to the sentence, either by making it the subject of the main clause that immediately follows the modifier or by turning the dangler into a clause that includes the missing noun phrase, noun, or pronoun.

> **Revised:** Exhausted from a long night of studying, *I* felt like the test would go on forever.

> **Revised:** Because *I* was exhausted from a long night of studying, the test seemed to go on forever.

> **Revised:** After eating five tacos, Mark thought a nap sounded like a good idea.

> **Revised:** After Mark had eaten five tacos, he thought a nap sounded like a good idea.

Notice that some revision of the main clause or modifier may be needed to accommodate the added noun or pronoun.

15.2 Parallel Structure

Parallel structure is a language pattern created through the repetition of word forms or grammatical elements. Parallel structure is commonly found in lists and comparisons, but it may also be used for a variety of purposes, including highlighting logical relationships, improving sentence clarity, creating rhythm, and adding emphasis.

Parallel Nouns: He is an outstanding *student*, *artist*, and *friend*.

Parallel Adjectives: It's the *smartest, funniest, bravest* book I've ever read.

Parallel Verbs: The thunder *rumbled* and *crashed* overhead.

Parallel Adjective Clauses: The team knows *that the competition is fierce* and *that the opposing team is impressive*.

Series Linked by a Coordinating Conjunction

Coordinating conjunctions (*for, and, nor, but, or, yet, so*) are used to join similar language elements, such as words, phrases, clauses, and sentences. In a list or series joined by a coordinating conjunction, all items in the series should be parallel to one another. If items are not parallel, the sentence may be awkward or unclear.

Awkward: The scientific process involves *asking questions, hypotheses,* and *conducting research*.

To maintain consistency in this sentence, we need to change the form of the second item in the series.

Parallel: The scientific process involves *asking questions, forming hypotheses,* and *conducting research*.

Series Linked by Correlative Conjunctions

Parallel structure is particularly important for maintaining clarity in sentences that use correlative conjunctions. Correlative conjunctions link two similarly structured words, phrases, or clauses in a sentence. Examples of correlative conjunction pairs include *either/or, neither/nor,* and *not only/but also*.

Awkward: For the final course assignment, students may *either* take a test *or* a paper.

To maintain consistency in this sentence, the phrase after each part of the correlative conjunction must use the same structure — in this case, a verb followed by its object.

Parallel: For the final course project, students may *either* take a test *or* write a paper.

Elements in a Comparison

When a sentence compares two or more items, the items being compared should be in parallel form. Nonparallel comparisons may be awkward or unclear.

Awkward: *Freewriting* is a less structured prewriting approach than *to outline*.

Parallel: *Freewriting* is a less structured prewriting approach than *outlining*.

Awkward: *Completing an assignment* in steps using the writing process is far easier than *to write an essay* in one sitting right before it's due.

Parallel: *Completing an assignment* in steps using the writing process is far easier than *writing an essay* in one sitting right before it's due.

15.3 Sentence Style

The first two sections in this chapter address common errors in sentence structure that can interfere with the clarity and flow of your sentences: misplaced modifiers and parallel structure. Eliminating these errors will ensure that your ideas are communicated clearly and your writing flows well. But polished prose is about more than just eliminating errors. Two ways you can make your essays more engaging are by using strong action verbs and by varying sentence length and types.

Action Verbs

It is impossible to construct a complete sentence without a verb, but the type of verb you use is up to you. You can use verbs that contain action, for example, *jump, cry, sing,* or *run.* Or you can use state-of-being verbs, such as *am, is, are, were,* which simply describe a static and unchanging condition:

- I am tall.
- Stan is hungry.
- It is cold.
- The children were asleep.

In each of the above sentences, the subject is motionless. When all of your subjects are static, your prose becomes sluggish. Although it is nearly impossible to write without using an occasional *am, is, are, was,* or *were,* the use of strong action verbs creates writing that is more vigorous and engaging:

- Greg slammed the ball over the fence.
- The heavy winds and flooding wreaked havoc in the small, coastal town.
- Dad incinerates his hamburgers when he grills.

If you're like most college freshmen, you use far more state-of-being verbs than action verbs, but that doesn't mean your sentences are incorrect. Replacing state-of-being verbs with strong action verbs simply makes your prose more engaging. Review the sentences in the table below, noticing how in the first sentence, the subject remains motionless, but in the second sentence, the subject performs an action.

No Action	*Action*
My instructor is very loud.	My instructor bellows when he lectures.
She is a good singer.	She croons like an angel.
My boss is suspicious of his employees.	My boss scrutinizes his employees' every move.

Another great benefit of using action verbs is that you can focus on using the strongest, most precise verb possible. Review the table below, and notice how each row contains verbs that all have the same definition. However, the verbs in the second column all have a slightly different, nuanced meaning.

Verb	Synonyms
To look	glare, stare, glance, gaze, examine, peep, scrutinize
To eat	devour, gobble, gorge, consume, nibble, gnaw, munch
To hold	grip, cuddle, embrace, squeeze, enfold, hug, clutch, grasp
To cry	scream, bellow, bawl, wail, holler, whimper
To walk	saunter, stroll, amble, stagger, strut, sashay, prance

Crafting essays that are not only correct but also engaging doesn't require a vivid imagination or a gift for writing. Any student can use action verbs to add vigor and style to their prose.

PRACTICE: Look over a past essay you have written. How many times did you use state-of-being verbs versus action verbs? Do you see opportunities for improvement? If so, practice incorporating this technique into your next essay.

Sentence Variety

Strong writing often incorporates a variety of sentence types that vary in length. No one type is more correct than another, but the most engaging prose uses a combination of all sentence types. If you use too many long sentences (compound, complex, compound-complex) your reader will feel overwhelmed and lose sight of what you are trying to say. On the other hand, if all of your sentences are short and choppy (simple, normal), your writing will feel rushed and unsophisticated. Alternating between lengths and types of sentences allows writers to use sentences strategically, emphasizing important points through short sentences and telling stories with longer ones. Varying sentence length also creates rhythm and increases interest.

Simple Sentences

A simple sentence contains a single main clause. It may also include modifiers.

Cara (S) *is studying* (V) for a chemistry exam.

The main clause in a simple sentence can have a compound subject.

Cara and Raul (S) *are studying* (V) for a chemistry exam.

It may also have a compound verb.

Raul (S) *is studying* (V) for a chemistry exam and *listening* (V) to music.

In addition, the main clause in a simple sentence can have an implied subject.

> Don't *wait* (V) until the last minute to study for the chemistry exam. (The implied but unstated subject of this sentence is *you*.)

Compound Sentences

A compound sentence contains two or more independent clauses, each with its own subject and verb. The clauses in a compound sentence can be joined by a coordinating conjunction.

> A new mushroom-shaped sea *animal* (S) *has been discovered* (V) near Australia, but *scientists* (S) *have not been able* (V) to classify it within existing categories of animal life.

The clauses of a compound sentence can also be joined by a semicolon, or by a semicolon followed by a conjunctive adverb such as *however*.

> A new mushroom-shaped sea *animal* (S) *has been discovered* (V) near Australia; however, *scientists* (S) *have not been able* (V) to classify it within existing categories of animal life.

Complex Sentences

A complex sentence contains one main clause and at least one subordinate clause.

> Luis volunteers every week at an animal shelter [main clause] because he wants to become a veterinarian [subordinate clause].

In some complex sentences, the word that connects the subordinate clause to the main clause may be implied.

> Musicians know [main clause] [that] hours of work are necessary to perfect their craft [subordinate clause].

Compound-Complex Sentences

A compound-complex sentence contains two or more main clauses and at least one subordinate clause.

> Although some students were nervous about learning computer programming [subordinate clause], most found the assignments interesting [main clause], and Rachel was inspired to learn more programming on her own [main clause].

Normal Sentences

The normal sentence is the most common sentence structure in English. Although a normal sentence may include modifiers, it always places a subject before a verb at the beginning of its main clause.

> The *teacher assigned* a new project on Monday.

Inverted Sentences

An inverted sentence reverses the subject-verb order of a normal English sentence so that all or part of the verb appears before the subject.

Deep in the heart of the forest *stands* (V) an ancient *tree* (S).

Cumulative Sentences

A cumulative sentence is composed of a main clause followed by a series of subordinate clauses or phrases that add information and detail.

They were best friends — always loyal, rarely apart, and absolutely inseparable.

Periodic Sentences

A periodic sentence ends with the main clause and begins with modifying phrases or clauses. The meaning of a periodic sentence may not be clear to the reader until the very end of the sentence.

By triumphing over a series of dangerous obstacles, standing bravely in the face of fear, and working together as a team, the heroes of the story will save the day.

Mixing Long and Short Sentences

The paragraph below illustrates how the overuse of long sentences can make writing confusing and dull.

In college, students often hear about the need to develop their critical thinking skills, but they don't always understand that critical thinking is the ability to approach learning by examining ideas in an organized and rational manner, or that those skills can be developed by going beneath the surface of ideas to gain a deeper understanding, which is especially important when those ideas represent viewpoints that differ from their own. Critical thinking also requires students to examine their most deeply held beliefs, and that makes them better writers because once they know that the ideas and beliefs that guide their actions and shape their thoughts can withstand scrutiny, they are empowered to write with conviction, and that makes their words resonate with authenticity, purpose, and meaning.

This entire paragraph is made up of only two sentences! These overly long sentences obscure the paragraph's main idea and make it just plain boring. While each clause does provide relevant information, readers may have difficulty following its logic or staying awake to the end. Now examine this paragraph, which has been written entirely in short sentences:

College students are often told they need to develop their critical thinking skills. Unfortunately, they don't always know what that means. Critical thinkers approach learning by examining ideas in an organized and rational manner. They go beyond the surface of ideas to gain a deeper understanding. This is especially important when those ideas represent viewpoints that differ from their own. Critical thinking also requires students to examine their most deeply held beliefs. This makes them better writers. Knowing the ideas and beliefs that guide their actions and shape their thoughts can withstand scrutiny empowers them to write with conviction. That makes their words resonate with authenticity, purpose, and meaning.

This paragraph uses the same information as the previous one but breaks it into nine sentences. While the information is far more digestible through these shorter sentences, the reader may not know what information is the most pertinent to the paragraph's purpose.

In the following paragraph, notice how the use of varying sentence lengths and types improves the clarity and vigor of this paragraph.

In college, students often hear that they need to develop their critical thinking skills, but they don't always know what that means. Critical thinkers approach learning by examining ideas in an organized and rational manner. Students can develop their ability to think critically by going beyond the surface of ideas to gain a deeper understanding, especially when those ideas explore viewpoints that differ from our own. Critical thinking also requires students to examine their most deeply held beliefs, and that makes them better writers. When students know that the ideas and beliefs that guide their actions and shape their thoughts can withstand scrutiny, they feel empowered to write with conviction. That sense of confidence makes their words resonate with authenticity, purpose, and meaning.

16

Word Choice

16.1 Appropriateness

Every time you communicate with someone, you make immediate, often instinctive language choices. When you text a good friend, for example, you might use shorthand such as *u* for "you," *omw* for "on my way," and *tbh* for "to be honest." You can be sure your friend not only understands what you write but also expects you to write in that style. However, you probably wouldn't use that same shorthand in an email to a teacher or in a job or college application because it would seriously diminish your chances of receiving a favorable response. Your choice of words — also known as diction — affects how others perceive you and in turn reflects how well you know your audience or recognize what is appropriate in a given circumstance.

Appropriate communication uses language suited to its purpose and appropriate for your audience. In any writing you do, you must pay close attention to the words you choose.

Tone

Tone is conveyed by word choice and indicates a writer's attitude toward his or her subject and audience. To communicate effectively, you must choose a tone appropriate for your topic, your purpose, and your audience. There are as many different tones as there are human emotions. Which tone you choose depends in large part on the purpose of your writing. Do you seek to inform, to persuade, or to entertain? Each purpose requires a different tone.

To create an appropriate tone, think about what kind of attitude would best accomplish your purpose with a particular audience. What are your audience's expectations?

Formality

Formal language is often used for professional or academic situations, or for topics the writer takes seriously. Formal language relies on sophisticated vocabulary. It avoids slang, colloquialisms, and clichés, as well as biased and exclusionary diction. It conveys a sincere and serious tone. Sentences are constructed in a clear and concise manner and contain no contractions. Do not confuse formal with stuffy or pretentious. Formal language does not mean you must encumber your writing with obscure words or long sentences that make reading difficult for your audience.

Informal language allows the writer more flexibility because it reflects the language and dialect used in everyday conversations. In informal writing situations, sentences tend to be shorter and simpler, vocabulary is not as sophisticated, and writing may include slang, clichés, and contractions. Additionally, the tone is more personal and friendly. Although you should use *always* use formal language in any writing for academic and professional purposes (including emails to professors and potential employers), informal language is perfectly suitable for personal correspondence and writing that seeks to entertain. Much of social media writing relies on informal language.

Jargon

Jargon refers to specialized language used by a group of people who share the same knowledge base. This specialized language operates in a large variety of groups, from skateboarders to cell biologists.

Jargon can be convenient and even necessary. A cell biologist writing an article for an academic journal can use terms such as *transfection* and *in silico* to succinctly express her argument and be confident that readers understand. However, using those terms without explaining their meaning in an article for a magazine aimed at a more general audience would likely leave readers confused and might even make them feel excluded.

Writers can avoid using jargon by being aware of their audience. When you write, ask yourself, *Will my audience understand this terminology or not?* When in doubt, choose straightforward, simple, and clear words. If your topic requires the use of specialized vocabulary, jargon may be unavoidable. For instance, in a research paper on genetically modified foods, you may need to discuss terms such as *genetic engineering* and *gene targeting*. In this case, explain each term as plainly and concisely as possible to ensure that your readers can follow your narrative.

Euphemisms

A euphemism is a word or phrase that replaces another term so as to render that term more palatable. Euphemisms attempt to beautify or conceal. For instance, rather than acknowledge the harsh reality of death, we might say that someone has *passed on*.

When we call a garbage collector a *sanitation engineer*, we are using a euphemism. In the best-case scenario, a euphemism can encourage a change in perspective. We can call attention to the hard work of collecting garbage and encourage respect for those who practice the profession by renaming them *sanitation engineers*. In the worst-case scenario, a euphemism covers up atrocities, such as the terms *collateral damage* for wartime civilian deaths or *ethnic cleansing* for genocide.

Because the purpose of a euphemism is to soften or conceal the harshness or reality of the thing it names, euphemisms by nature reflect vague language and can cause readers to interpret terms in wildly differing ways. To avoid euphemisms, use precise language.

Slang

Slang refers to language shared by a particular group of people. Musicians keep to a beat by *staying in the pocket*, and gamers might talk about *owning* (dominating) their opponents. Although slang can provide vibrant dialogue, it should be avoided in formal writing for several reasons. First, slang excludes readers who do not understand the vocabulary. Second, slang is mercurial—phrases or words usually remain current only for a few years. For example, a guitarist's excellent skills might be described as *groovy, far-out, cool, awesome*, or *sick*. Each adjective dates the language to a particular time and often pins it to a specific group or geographic area. Using precise and standard vocabulary instead of slang ensures that readers will clearly and easily understand the writing.

Biased and Exclusionary Language

Students come from a wide variety of backgrounds, and that often influences the way they speak and write. To become an effective communicator, you must learn to be sensitive to those differences and avoid language that is divisive, offensive, or demeaning. You should also avoid using the pronouns *them, they*, or *those people* to refer to groups who do not share your background or ethnicity.

Although this sounds like a lesson in political correctness, it is more about the art of discourse and how to disagree productively. If you want your audience to accept your viewpoint or give careful consideration to your ideas, you should strive to establish common ground and avoid emphasizing your differences. That will allow your audience to focus on your ideas alone and not the ways in which you differ.

Use language that is gender-neutral.

Avoid	Use Instead
businessman	business executive
chairman	chairperson
female astronaut	astronaut
female doctor	doctor
forefathers	ancestors
foreman	supervisor
mailman	mail carrier
male nurse	nurse
man, mankind	person, people, our species, humanity
manmade	synthetic
policeman	police officer
salesman	sales representative

Here are some other tips for avoiding biased and exclusionary language.

- Avoid naming a person's race unless doing so is relevant to the main of idea of your essay. When you do refer to a person's race, use the preferred term. Preferred terms tend to change over time, so do not assume that something that was printed in the past is still an acceptable usage. A quick online search can help guide you on what term is currently the most inclusive one to use.

- Avoid derogatory terms associated with age, such as *little old lady* or *the elderly*. Instead, use the phrase *a ninety-year-old woman* or *senior citizens*. Instead of *teenybopper* or *immature adolescent*, use the term *teenager* or *teen*.

- Avoid political terminology that has negative connotations: *radical, left-wing, right-wing*. Use of these words may feel like criticism to anyone who identifies with its associated party.

- Avoid words like *fanatical, cult,* or *fundamentalist* when referring to a religion.

- Avoid phrases like *confined to a wheelchair* and *victim of* (a disease) because these terms draw unnecessary attention to a person's disability or illness. Instead, use the phrase *someone who uses a wheelchair* and *person with* (a disease).

- Avoid referring to a person's sexual orientation unless doing so is relevant to your essay's main idea and do your best to refer to people by their preferred pronouns.

16.2 Exact Words

Words are a writer's tools. Choosing the correct tool for the task allows a writer to communicate effectively. An imprecise word choice, however, can derail a writing task and leave readers confused and frustrated.

The *sufficient* server brought menus and took our orders quickly.

Sufficient means "adequate" or "enough," but the more effective word in this context is *efficient*. Because the server takes the orders quickly, we know he is more than adequate—he is skilled. The words *efficient* and *sufficient* not only sound alike, but are close in meaning. Choosing precise words is a skill that writers practice to improve their craft.

Connotation and Denotation

Words can have both connotative and denotative meanings. The denotation of a word is its literal definition. The words *home, residence, abode,* and *domicile* all share the same denotation. They all refer to the place where someone lives. But we say "Home is where the heart is," not "The residence is where the heart is" for a good reason: The word *home* carries connotations of belonging, relaxation, and security. Connotations indicate emotional or cultural associations and can suggest positive or negative overtones.

Denotative: *Celebrity photographers take pictures* of the rich and famous.

Connotative: The *paparazzi hound* the rich and famous.

In the above example, *celebrity photographers* is denotative and describes a profession matter-of-factly, while *paparazzi* evokes a negative connotation and transforms professionals into parasites exploiting their targets.

Knowing the different connotations of words allows you a greater proficiency in conveying tone and more precision in description.

Clichés

A cliché can make your writing as *dull as a doorknob*. A cliché is a phrase or saying that has been used so many times it no longer offers meaningful or fresh language that engages the reader.

When a writer uses a cliché, readers may pass over it because they've seen and heard those words so often. Precise, detailed, and fresh communication is necessary to keep readers' attention.

Some common clichés include:

- *Absence makes the heart grow fonder.*
- *first and foremost*
- *Beauty is in the eye of the beholder.*
- *in any way, shape, or form*
- *leave no stone unturned*
- *glass half-full / glass half-empty*
- *Blood is thicker than water.*
- *going forward*
- *Absolute power corrupts absolutely.*
- *tried and true*
- *the bottom line*
- *adding insult to injury*

To avoid using clichés, diagnose your own writing and find the clichés you rely on. If you favor the phrase *first and foremost*, use the search function in your document and either delete the phrase or replace it with a precise word choice. When you find a cliché in your writing, ask yourself how you can describe or explain something more clearly and precisely in your own words.

Idioms

An idiom is an expression or phrase peculiar to a particular group or area. Idioms tend to consist of conversational language and are more often used in informal writing than in academic writing. Idioms can enrich writing by adding local color. For instance, in the case of ordering a carbonated beverage, someone from the northeastern United States orders a "soda," someone in the South orders a "Coke" (no matter what brand the soft drink is), and a customer in the Midwest asks for a "pop." However, if your readers are not familiar with a particular idiom, you risk confusing your audience.

Idiomatic expressions rely on certain words in a certain order and only retain their meaning if used correctly. Pay close attention to the prepositions and articles in an idiomatic expression. If you write that your ninety-two-year-old neighbor *kicked the bucket*, your readers know that your neighbor died. However, if you write that your neighbor "kicked a bucket," your readers will wonder why your neighbor was angry. If you relax and *let off steam* by exercising, be sure you don't confuse yourself with a teapot by writing that you "let out steam."

Specific versus General

When it comes to word choice, the more specific, the better. The more specific you are when describing a noun, the more likely you are to control what your reader is picturing. For instance, if you ask twenty people to imagine a car without giving them any other specific instructions, each person will picture something different. However, if you ask your audience to imagine a red 2019 Corvette convertible, you are more likely to create a common image in the mind of your audience.

The table below illustrates how the more specific language is, the more effective and precise it is.

	Person	*Place*	*Thing*
General	Woman	Beach	Accessory
Specific	Older woman	Beach in Florida	Purse
More Specific	My sweet, gray-haired, eighty-two-year-old neighbor with laughing, blue eyes	The dazzling, white crystal sand of St. Pete Beach in Florida	A red Dooney & Bourke pebble grain zip satchel

Effective use of specific language allows writers to share with their audience what they are seeing, hearing, tasting, feeling, or smelling. Although all successful writers have mastered the ability to skillfully manipulate what their readers experience, even beginning writers can incorporate the use of specific word choice to become more effective communicators.

Punctuation

17.1 End Punctuation

Periods

The most common use of a period is to signal the end of a declarative sentence. A declarative sentence makes an assertion.

> Sarah will pilot the plane.

A period should appear at the end of a sentence that includes an indirect question. An indirect question conveys the idea of a question without asking it directly, typically by stating that a question was or is being asked.

> Julio asked if Sarah will pilot the plane.

A period can also indicate that the word preceding it has been abbreviated, or shortened. When an abbreviation ends a sentence, follow it with just one period.

> Sarah G. Stein will fly the plane at 10:00 P.M., and the flight lasts for two hours.

Abbreviations of units of time or measurement also use periods. However, most organizational names (PTA for Parent Teacher Association), place names — such as countries (USA for United States of America); airports (LGA for LaGuardia Airport); and states (NY for New York) — and people's names (MLK Jr. for Martin Luther King Jr.) are abbreviated with capital letters without periods.

Question Marks

Use a question mark to signal the end of a direct question. A direct question asks for information. It might ask for a yes or no response, elicit information, or echo a statement in question form.

> Where will the plane land?

Sometimes a direct question can express doubt, irony, or sarcasm.

Sarah will pilot the plane?

Avoid using question marks to signal doubt in formal writing by rephrasing the indirect question as a declarative sentence (for example, *I was unaware that Sarah is qualified to pilot a plane*.). You should also avoid using question marks that express irony and sarcasm; instead, express your thoughts directly (for example, *Sarah's dubious talent for flying aircraft makes me hesitant to take this trip*.).

Exclamation Points

An exclamation point can interject, create emphasis, and express strong emotion. Inserting one at the end of a sentence will change the tone — and sometimes the meaning — of a given assertion, question, or command.

Oh no! This is horrible! I can't believe this happened! Our vacation is ruined!

Tornado! Find shelter!

It is best to use exclamation points sparingly, especially in formal writing, and *never* use more than one at a time or in combination with other punctuation (for example, *Really?!?!*) as you might in a text or informal writing.

17.2 Commas

The comma indicates a pause within a sentence, much like the act of taking a breath while in conversation. The separations commas create between words, phrases, and clauses affect the meaning of your sentences. By clearly delineating both concepts and objects in what would otherwise be a wall of text, commas help your readers follow your train of thought with ease. When deciding whether to use a comma, keep the following tips in mind.

DO Use a Comma with a Coordinating Conjunction to Join Two Main Clauses

To join two main clauses together in a single complete sentence, place a comma after the first clause and before a coordinating conjunction (*and, but, for, or, nor, yet*).

Jaime doesn't have a big kitchen in his apartment, but he still manages to cook delicious meals for his family.

When using a coordinating conjunction to link two phrases, or a phrase and a clause, do not add a comma.

Incorrect: Tasha sang, and clapped her hands.

Correct: Tasha sang and clapped her hands.

DO Use a Comma after an Introductory Clause, Phrase, or Word

Use a comma after an introductory phrase, clause, or word at the beginning of a sentence.

Smiling, Danez offered his hand for me to shake.

Before today, I'd never seen the ocean.

While Morgan chops the celery, I'll wash the tomatoes.

You may omit a comma after an introductory word or short phrase if there is no chance a reader could misinterpret your meaning.

Someday soon I'll find the perfect prom dress.

DO Use a Comma to Separate Items in a Series

When listing three or more items in a series, separate each item with a comma. The series might consist of single words.

I baked pie, brownies, and cupcakes.

The items in the series might also consist of phrases or clauses.

I baked a juicy apple pie, chocolate brownies with peanut butter chips, and those cupcakes you like so much.

Some writers omit the comma before the final item in a series. This practice is common in journalism. However, leaving off the final comma in a series can obscure the meaning of a sentence, which is never desirable.

Unclear: After we left the ballgame, I met my parents, Anna and Joel.

In the sentence above, Anna and Joel could be the writer's parents. If Anna and Joel are two more people joining the writer and his or her parents after the ballgame, a comma is necessary for clarification.

Clear: After we left the ballgame, I met my parents, Anna, and Joel.

Remember that it is never wrong to place a comma before the last item in a series, and this practice is typically preferred in academic writing.

DO Use a Comma between Coordinate Adjectives

Coordinate adjectives function independently of each other in a sentence but still modify the same noun. In practice, if you remove one coordinate adjective from a sentence, the meaning of the sentence will not change significantly.

Use a comma to separate two or more coordinate adjectives. However, be careful not to use a comma after the final coordinate adjective.

Incorrect: He was a charismatic, likable, man.

Correct: He was a charismatic, likable man.

However, if you link coordinate adjectives with a coordinating conjunction (usually *and*), you should omit commas.

My bedroom is neat and clean and uncluttered.

Cumulative adjectives modify each other and the noun to which they all refer. The meaning of a cumulative adjective is typically objective, a quality most observers would agree on. Do not use a comma between cumulative adjectives.

He was a young Japanese man.

Applying two tests, the conjunction test and the order test, can help determine whether you are looking at coordinate or cumulative adjectives.

Coordinate adjectives can be joined by the conjunction *and* with natural-sounding results.

Clear: He was a charismatic and likable man.

Attempting to join cumulative adjectives with *and* will sound less than natural and possibly alter the meaning of the sentence.

Unclear: He was a young and Japanese man.

The order of coordinate adjectives can also be reversed with natural-sounding results.

Clear: He was a likable and charismatic man.

Attempting to reverse cumulative adjectives will sound less than natural and possibly alter the meaning of the sentence.

Unclear: He was a Japanese and young man.

Still not sure what kind of adjective you're dealing with? Here's one last clue: Cumulative adjectives typically stack according to meaning and in the following order: size, shape, condition/age, color, origin/material.

DO Use Commas to Set Off a Nonrestrictive Phrase or Clause

Place a comma both before and after nonrestrictive modifiers that fall midsentence. These phrases or clauses, sometimes called parenthetical modifiers, give nonessential information about the things they describe. However much they enhance a noun's meaning, nonrestrictive modifiers are not grammatically essential to that noun's definition in a particular context.

Tolkien's writing, which is now celebrated throughout the world, was once less mainstream.

Do not place a comma on either side of a restrictive modifier that falls midsentence. Restrictive modifiers are phrases or clauses that give essential information about the things they describe. They not only enhance the meaning of a noun phrase but also focus that meaning to a narrower subset.

All the fantasy novels that I have read seem influenced by Tolkien's work.

Generally, the relative pronoun *that* introduces a restrictive phrase, whereas the relative pronoun *which* introduces a nonrestrictive phrase. However, it is more succinct and often preferable to delete *that* or *which* from your own writing wherever their absence does not obscure meaning.

DO Use Commas to Set Off Nonrestrictive Appositives

An appositive is a noun or noun phrase that renames or adds information to the entity it modifies, usually another noun phrase. Two nouns used in apposition usually sit adjacent to each other. Like modifiers, appositives can be either restrictive or nonrestrictive. Nonrestrictive appositives can be removed from a sentence without changing the essential meaning of that sentence. Place a comma before and after a nonrestrictive appositive.

The author of "The Monsters and the Critics," J. R. R. Tolkien, studied language and culture.

Restrictive appositives, which cannot be removed from a sentence without changing its meaning, stand without commas.

The fantasy author J. R. R. Tolkien studied language and culture.

DO Use Commas to Set Off Conjunctive Adverbs

Use commas to set off conjunctive adverbs such as *accordingly*, *eventually*, and *furthermore*. The adverb might take a comma after, before, or on either side, depending on where it falls. When a conjunctive adverb falls in the middle of a clause, place a comma both before and after it.

He gave up on eating cupcakes, eventually, after several unpleasant trips to the dentist.

DO Use Commas to Set Off Parenthetical Expressions

A parenthetical expression is a short phrase or clause that appears within, and interrupts, another phrase or clause. It functions as an aside to your readers, and it can be set off from the rest of the sentence with commas. It can also be set off using parentheses.

My mother was, unlike last year, very pleased with the gift I gave her for her birthday.

DO Use Commas to Set Off a Phrase or Clause Expressing Contrast

Use commas to set off a phrase or clause that expresses contrast. Such phrases often contain a coordinating or subordinating conjunction that signals the contrasting relationship.

Whereas Georgia reads books, Ben prefers reading magazines.

Short contrasting phrases beginning with *but* don't always require commas.

Ben reads magazines but not books.

DO Use Commas to Set Off an Absolute Phrase

A comma links an absolute phrase to the rest of the sentence it modifies. An absolute phrase is a modifier attached to a sentence without the use of a conjunction. The comma may fall before, after, or on either side of an absolute phrase, depending where the phrase is placed within the sentence.

Being the champion bookworm of her school, Georgia read the contents of the entire library in just two years.

In the above sentence, the comma falls after the introductory absolute phrase.
Here, the absolute phrase falls between two coordinate clauses and is set off with commas on either side.

Ben considered having pizza for lunch, his mouth watering at the thought of gooey melted cheese, but he decided to have a sandwich instead.

DO Use Commas to Set Off a Direct Quotation

Use commas to introduce dialogue and to set off direct quotations in which words, phrases, or sentences are copied word for word from another source. Always place the comma after the last word before the opening quotation mark. To interrupt a quotation with phrases such as *she said*, set off the interrupting phrase or clause with commas.

As my grandmother always said, "A little hard work never hurt anybody, but I'm not taking my chances."

"I know you don't like basketball very much," Seth said, "but I still think you'd enjoy watching a live NBA game."

However, you may omit the comma before very short quotations or quotations introduced by conjunctions such as *that* or *whether*.

When James asked Adriana to the prom, her answer was "maybe."

She said that she "wanted some privacy."

You also omit a comma when the quotation reads as part of your own sentence, as in a restrictive appositive.

The saying "wherever you go, there you are" always makes me smile.

DO Use Commas around *Yes* and *No*, Mild Interjections, Tag Questions, and the Name or Title of Someone Directly Addressed

Set off an introductory *yes* or *no* with a comma.

No, he did not plan on going to the ball.

Interjections that don't require other punctuation, such as an exclamation point or question mark, are set off with commas.

And then, Lord have mercy, who walked in but your father.

A tag question at the end of a declarative or imperative sentence transforms it into a question. Introduce the tag question with a comma.

He said he was going, didn't he?

Place a comma before a name or title used in direct address.

Please come to the ball, Prince Charming.

DO Use Commas to Set Off Dates, States, Countries, and Addresses

Use a comma to set off the year in a full date, even when it falls midsentence.

He was born on January 21, 1993, the day after President Bill Clinton's inauguration.

However, omit the comma when only the month and year are given.

He was born in January 1993.

Place commas around the name of a state when the name of a city precedes it, whether the state is spelled out or abbreviated. However, omit the comma if the state's name stands alone.

She has lived in Sacramento, California, for the past fifteen years.

She has lived in California for the past fifteen years.

Set off the name of a country with a comma when the name of a state or other internal region precedes it, but omit the comma if the country's name stands alone.

I'd like to visit Bern, Switzerland, before I die.

I'd like to visit Switzerland before I die.

Place a comma around the different parts of an address, except between the state and zip code.

They work at 175 Fifth Ave., New York, NY 10010.

DO NOT Use a Comma to Separate a Subject from Its Verb or a Verb from Its Object

Never place a comma between a subject and its main verb.

Incorrect: She, makes books all day long.

Correct: She makes books all day long.

Never place a comma between a verb and its object.

Incorrect: She makes, books all day long.

Correct: She makes books all day long.

DO NOT Use a Comma to Divide a Compound Subject or Predicate

In cases in which a conjunction such as *and* creates a compound subject, never divide that subject by placing a comma before or after the conjunction.

Incorrect: Gabby, and Steve saw me trip on the sidewalk.

Correct: Gabby and Steve saw me trip on the sidewalk.

Don't separate the components of a compound predicate.

Incorrect: The ballerinas leapt, and pirouetted, and pointed their feet.

Correct: The ballerinas leapt and pirouetted and pointed their feet.

17.3 Semicolons

A semicolon conveys a closer connection than a period but a stronger break than a comma between two sentence elements. It usually coordinates more complex sentence elements, such as independent clauses within a compound sentence. Though the semicolon was used more freely in past eras, its function within clauses has narrowed over time to a few widely accepted uses. Generally speaking, it's best to use semicolons infrequently.

Using Semicolons with Conjunctions

A semicolon joins two independent clauses not linked by a coordinating or subordinating conjunction.

Gabby and Steve tried not to laugh; they couldn't help themselves.

Using Semicolons with Conjunctive Adverbs

Like conjunctions, conjunctive adverbs join two independent clauses, but they do so with an adverbial emphasis. Conjunctive adverbials include summarizing words such as *thus*, indicators of time such as *finally*, and contrasting words or phrases such as *however*, *nevertheless*, and *to the contrary*. Place a semicolon between two independent clauses linked by a conjunctive adverb.

Gabby and Steve tried not to laugh; nevertheless, they couldn't help themselves.

Using Semicolons with Items in a Series

When one or more of the items in a series contains internal punctuation, or is long and complex, using a semicolon to delineate each group of items helps clarify the sentence.

The vacation package my parents bought includes a round-trip flight; complimentary breakfast, lunch, and dinner every day at the hotel; and organized day trips such as snorkeling, hiking, and fishing.

17.4 Colons

Colons indicate a close relationship between a clause and what follows. The clause that comes after a colon often clarifies what precedes it. Using a colon can also signal some form of introduction or amplification, such as the introduction of a list, series, appositive, or another independent clause. This use serves the same purpose as using "namely" or "as follows" to introduce a list.

The workshop on using outside sources focused on three main concepts: quoting, paraphrasing, and summarizing.

With rare exception, a colon is placed after an independent clause, but not after a phrase or dependent clause. In general, avoid using a colon where it disrupts a sentence that could otherwise stand on its own.
Do NOT use a colon between a verb and its object.

Incorrect: Last Halloween, I saw: three ghouls, five superheroes, and one Mad Hatter.

Correct: Last Halloween, I saw a variety of costumes: three ghouls, five superheroes, and one Mad Hatter.

Avoid using a colon between a preposition and its object.

Incorrect: Last Halloween, I got candy from: an old lady in an empty mansion and her tenant in the shed out back.

Correct: Last Halloween, I got candy from some interesting neighbors: the weirdest were the old lady in an empty mansion and her tenant in the shed out back.

Do NOT use a colon before a list introduced by *such as*.

Incorrect: I prefer healthy snacks, such as: apples, oranges, mangoes, and pecans.

Correct: I prefer healthy snacks: apples, oranges, mangoes, and pecans.

Using a Colon between Two Main Clauses

Place a colon between two main clauses where the second clause exemplifies, explains, amplifies, or summarizes the first.

Writing is like driving at night: You only need to see a few feet ahead to reach your destination.

Using Colons with a List or Series

The colon may introduce a list or series.

Spring is my favorite time of year for the following reasons: mild temperatures, lots of sunshine, and many fragrant blossoms.

Using Colons with Appositives

A colon preceded by a main clause can introduce an appositive, a phrase that renames or identifies another noun.

Mary was determined to overcome her worst habit: binge-watching horror movies.

Using Colons with Quotations

A colon can introduce a long or heavily punctuated quotation.

Vincent van Gogh said: "I have tried to emphasize that those people, eating their potatoes in the lamplight, have dug the earth with those very hands they put in the dish, and so it speaks of 'manual labour,' and how they have honestly earned their food."

Conventional Colon Uses

Use a colon rather than a comma after a salutation in a formal letter.

To whom it may concern:

Use a colon within biblical citations.

Matthew 17:20

Use a colon between a text's title and subtitle.

Transformational Grammar: A First Course

Use a colon between the publisher's state and name when citing a primary source such as a book in academic writing.

Fine, Ruth. *Procession: The Art of Norman Lewis.* University of California Press, 2015.

Use a colon between the hour and minutes when giving the time of day with numerals.

2:22 P.M.

17.5 Em Dashes and Hyphens

Em Dashes

The em dash, often referred to as the dash, is a versatile punctuation mark that signals a rupture in a sentence's logic or syntax. It is called an "em dash" because it takes up the same amount of space as the capital letter "M." It often sets off an amplifying or explanatory element within a clause. Its role can be similar to that of commas, parentheses, or colons, but the dash conveys a sharper emphasis than its cousins, underscoring the disruptive nature of what follows. It often signals an abrupt shift in tone or break in thought. Use the em dash sparingly.

Surely he'd be home soon — but no, it was karaoke night!

You may use an em dash to introduce an expression, amplifying phrase, series, or appositive.

There's only one song I'll sing — "Brother, Can You Spare a Dime?"

Em dashes may also set off an emphatic aside or a parenthetical expression from the rest of the sentence.

And then — even though I had already lost my voice! — I tried to get on stage and sing a Beyoncé song.

Note that the interjected phrase contains its own internal punctuation in the preceding sentence. A question mark or exclamation point may punctuate interruptive phrases set off by em dashes.

Hyphens

In Hollywood, an actor who produces his own film becomes a "hyphenate": an actor-producer. If she also directs, she's an actor-producer-director. Even beyond Hollywood, the simple hyphen is a way to make a single word out of two or more words.

One helping dog is Hasty, who is not your *run-of-the-mill* golden retriever: He can locate avalanche victims.

At Lake Nakuru in Kenya, you can get an *awe-inspiring* view of thousands of pink flamingos feeding on the lake's plentiful algae.

Spud Webb was only five feet seven inches tall when he *slam-dunked* over the reigning champion to win the 1986 NBA dunk contest.

As in the first two sentences, hyphenated words are often adjectives, but they may be nouns or verbs (as in the third sentence).

Hyphens have four common uses:

- To create compound words from two or more words
- To write numbers from twenty-one to ninety-nine and fractions, such as one-fourth
- To add certain prefixes to words, such as *self-imposed* or *pre-Columbian*
- To span time, distance, or other quantities

The following examples will give you more details about how to use hyphens precisely and correctly.

Hyphens in Compound Words

A compound word is most commonly a word formed from two or more separate words put together.

down + hearted = downhearted

fire + works = fireworks

key + board = keyboard

A compound word can also be made of two words commonly used together. The two words in the phrase remain separate but function as one.

cloud nine   stock market   vice president

Compound words are also formed from two or more words joined by a hyphen or hyphens.

mother-in-law   decision-maker   self-esteem

A hyphen may also be used in a compound word that has one or more elements beginning with a capital letter.

pre-Enlightenment   Picasso-like   half-Mexican, half-Chilean

Hyphens in Compound Adjectives

What do the hyphenated words in the following sentence have in common?

Women's basketball has seen many *record-breaking* athletes who dazzled with *high-scoring* games and *last-second* shots.

All three hyphenated words function as *adjectives*. Although hyphenated words can function as other parts of speech, they are often adjectives with special rules for punctuation.

Compound adjectives **preceding** the noun they modify should be hyphenated.

At six feet tall, Seimone Augustus has such great *ball-handling* skills that she had *double-digit* scores in almost all of her *high school* games.

Compound adjectives **following** the noun they modify should **not** be hyphenated.

In the WNBA, Augustus continues to display her skills at *ball handling*, with her regular-season scoring average in *double digits*.

The adverb *well*, when paired with an adjective, follows the same hyphenation rules as adjectives in the previous example.

Augustus is *well known* for continuing her *well-executed* shooting in playoff games after the regular season is over.

How do you hyphenate a series of compound words when they all have the same second word? Omit that word in all but the last adjective of the series.

Augustus was equally skilled in making *one-, two-, and three-point* shots.

Do not use a hyphen to link an adverb ending in *-ly* with an adjective.

In playoff games, Augustus's scoring has been *extremely consistent* with her average of nineteen points per game.

Prefixes and Suffixes

Prefixes and suffixes are elements added to a word to refine or change its meaning. An element added at the beginning of a root word is a *prefix*; one at the end is a *suffix*. Some prefixes and suffixes require hyphens.

A hyphen is always used after the prefixes *all-, ex-,* and *self-* and before the suffix *-elect*.

Several presidents had *self-limited* terms, declining to run again, although as *ex-president*, Teddy Roosevelt regretted his decision and tried to make a comeback.

In 1944, FDR made the *all-important* decision to run for a fourth term and was soon *president-elect*, but he served less than three months of that final term.

A hyphen can also be used where the added prefix/suffix makes pronunciation of the word confusing.

Theodore Roosevelt was not only a *far-ranging explorer* but also the first president to ride in an automobile.

Numbers

Numbers, when spelled out, use a hyphen in two cases: fractions and the compound whole numbers from twenty-one to ninety-nine. This applies to the adjective form of numbers as well.

Lyndon Johnson, the *thirty-sixth* president, was elected in 1964 with *three-fifths* of the vote, the widest margin in history, but he chose not to run again in 1968.

A hyphen should be used to indicate a span of time, distance, or other quantities.

If you get a paperback copy of President Kennedy's *Profiles in Courage*, you can read about President John Quincy Adams on pages *29-50*.

The workshop on punctuation will be held from *2:00-3:00* P.M. in the library.

The Great Depression spanned an entire decade, from *1929-1939*.

17.6 Parentheses

Parentheses are a pair of punctuation marks that set off extra information given within a sentence, such as an aside, explanation, or amplification. This type of expression is often called parenthetical.

Parentheses function much as the dash and comma do, but unlike the dash, they downplay the material they contain, and unlike the comma, they may contain text with no particular grammatical relationship to the rest of the sentence.

Parentheses can add a qualification, a date in time, or a brief explanation.

She preferred the company of doves (as opposed to that of sparrows).

You may use parentheses around letters or numbers enumerating items in a series, especially when that series is run into the main text (rather than displayed in a vertical list).

The Audubon Society's website described habitats for (1) doves, (2) sparrows, (3) mockingbirds, and (4) blue jays, much to her delight.

17.7 Apostrophes

Apostrophes have two main uses: to show possession and to indicate the omission of one or more letters, as in contractions. On rare occasions, they are also used to make a noun plural.

Contractions

Use an apostrophe in a contraction in place of the missing letter or letters.

The contraction for *does not* is *doesn't*.

The contraction for *would not* is *wouldn't*.

The contraction for *it is* is *it's*.

The contraction for *cannot* is *can't*.

Possessives

Using an apostrophe to show possession can be confusing. First, it is not always clear if a noun needs to be possessive. You make a noun possessive to show that something belongs to someone.

the girl's mittens = the mittens that belong to the girl

Joey's new car = the car that belongs to Joey

You can determine whether a noun should be possessive by substituting a possessive pronoun (his, her, its, their) in place of the noun in question. If you can do so, you must use the possessive form of the noun.

the girl's mittens = her mittens

Joey's new car = his new car

Second, whether to use an apostrophe and an "s" or an apostrophe alone depends on the type of noun you are making possessive. Even if the singular form of the noun ends in "s" (*cactus, cosmos, walrus*), you must still use an apostrophe and an "s." The same holds true for proper nouns that end in "s" (*Texas, Christmas, James, Mars*).

> Mrs. Jones's office
>
> Aeschylus's plays
>
> Texas's economy

Plural Nouns

Plural nouns also use an apostrophe and an "s."

> children's playground
>
> women's rights
>
> your teeth's roots

The only time you use an apostrophe alone to make a noun possessive is for plural nouns that end in "s" or "es."

> two actresses' roles
>
> girls' dormitories
>
> roses' fragrance
>
> trees' root systems

Care must be taken when making proper nouns that end in "s" plural and possessive. For example, if you are a guest of the Jones family, you are one of the Joneses' guests. The plural of Jones is Joneses.

When two people possess the same item, use an apostrophe and an "s" after the second name only.

> Leonard and Bella's new home is beautiful.
>
> My mom and dad's new RV is bigger than my apartment.

To show that ownership is separate, use the possessive form for both.

> Tammy's and Maddie's homes are both lovely.
>
> The Joneses' and the Wilsons' yards are always the best in the neighborhood.

Plural Nouns

Apostrophes should not be used to make regular nouns, dates, numbers, capital letters, or most abbreviations plural. The few exceptions are when an apostrophe is necessary to avoid confusion, for instance, with lowercase letters, with words that are used as nouns, and with abbreviations that contain periods.

Apostrophe needed:

My grandmother was always reminding me to cross my t's and dot my i's.

When the referendum was put to a vote, it received far more yes's than no's.

There were more Ph.D.'s at the neuroscience conference than laypeople.

NO apostrophe needed:

Don't forget to include your URLs with your bibliographic entries.

The houses in that neighborhood are priced in the high 400s.

Styles for women changed drastically during the 1920s.

DO NOT use an apostrophe with possessive pronouns (hers, ours, yours, theirs).

Incorrect: That beverage is hers'.

Correct: That beverage is hers.

Mechanics

18.1 Capital Letters

What's the difference between Mark Twain, author of *Tom Sawyer*, and the mark you got on your last math test? One Mark is capitalized, and the other isn't.

Vacationers might visit a grand canyon in Puerto Rico, but they can visit the Grand Canyon only in Arizona.

In general, names of specific persons, places, and things are capitalized. These names are known grammatically as proper nouns. General persons, places, and things (common nouns) are not capitalized.

Adjectives made from proper nouns (like "*Puerto Rican* vacation") are also capitalized. The following examples will give you more details about when to capitalize words.

Proper Nouns

A *proper noun* is a word that names a unique person, place, event, or thing. Proper nouns should be capitalized.

- Philadelphia
- Exxon
- Beyoncé

If a name contains more than one word, each word is capitalized, though minor words within these names (for example *of*, *in*, and *the*) are not.

- Mexico City
- *Raiders of the Lost Ark*
- Thomas Jefferson

Adjective forms of proper nouns are also capitalized.

- Exxon-like
- Jeffersonian
- Kafkaesque

Title or Rank

A title or rank preceding a proper noun should be capitalized.

President Kennedy had a mixed-breed dog named Pushinka, a gift from *Premier* Nikita Khrushchev of the Soviet Union.

However, titles that precede common nouns usually are not capitalized.

Dwight D. Eisenhower, commanding *general* in World War II and *president* before Kennedy, had a parakeet named Gabby.

Although the abbreviation of an academic or professional degree (*M.D., Ph.D.*) is always capitalized, the full name (*doctor of medicine, doctor of philosophy*) is not.

Family Relationships

A family relationship (sister, nephew, grandfather, and so on) should only be capitalized when it is part of a proper name, or when it substitutes for a proper name.

Eleanor Roosevelt often referred to President Theodore Roosevelt as her "Uncle Ted." [Here, *Uncle* is part of a proper name, *Ted*.]

The Roosevelt children soon learned that *Granny*, Eleanor's mother-in-law, would give them anything they wanted. [Here, *Granny* substitutes for the grandmother's proper name.]

In fact, Eleanor's *mother-in-law* encouraged her *grandchildren* to think of her as their real *mother*! [Here, the family relationship does not function as a proper name.]

Religious Names

Names of religions and deities, along with the words denoting the followers of a religion, should be capitalized.

Singapore is one of the most religiously diverse countries in the world, with large numbers of people who follow *Buddhism*, *Christianity*, and *Islam*.

About 5 percent of Singaporeans are Hindu, who worship such divinities as *Vishnu* and *Shiva*.

While more than 800,000 citizens of Singapore are *Muslim*, fewer than 6,000 are *Jewish*.

Place Names

Proper nouns that name a geographic place, region, or feature should be capitalized.

- Paris, France
- the Northeast
- the Rockies
- Yellowstone National Park
- Central Europe
- Niagara Falls

If the proper noun is a phrase, minor words such as *of* and *the* are not capitalized.

Garden of the Gods is a national park in Colorado.

Directional words, such as *north, south, east, west, northwest*, are capitalized if they are part of a place name. Otherwise they are not capitalized.

The team bus traveled *east* from Ohio to get to the game in *West Virginia*.

A common noun that is part of a place name is capitalized.

Yonge Street in Toronto, according to some, is the longest *street* in the world.

Days of the Week, Months, and Holidays

Days of the week, months, and holidays are capitalized. Seasons and academic terms are not capitalized.

This year, many students will celebrate the end of the *spring semester* on *Thursday, May* 24, just before leaving for the *Memorial Day* holiday.

Historical Events, Periods, and Documents

A historical event is a specific happening in history; it's not just any revolution, but the *American Revolution* or the *Russian Revolution*. Some time periods or eras in history are known by a name. In the United States, the 1920s were called the *Roaring Twenties*.

Historical events, periods, and documents should be capitalized.

- World War II
- the U.S. Constitution
- the Gilded Age
- D-Day
- the Revolutionary War

The exception to this rule is when the event or period is referred to not by a name but by a phrase.

- the reign of Louis XIV
- the American war for independence

Some events may be known by a single name, which is capitalized. When the term is used in a more general sense, it is not capitalized.

After the *Revolution*, many people in the new United States wanted George Washington to become king.

The twentieth century saw one *revolution* after another in African nations that had been colonies of European powers.

Names of Institutions

An institution is an entity such as a school, government, or business. Names of institutions should be capitalized, except for minor words such as *of* and *the*.

- Howard University
- Bank of America
- Federal Bureau of Investigation

In addition to names of schools and colleges, names of departments and specific courses should also be capitalized. Notice in the example below the difference between capitalized names and common nouns.

My local junior *college*, Winslow County Community *College*, has a number of excellent departments.

After talking to some faculty in the *Department of Natural Sciences*, I signed up for *Introduction to Biology*.

Titles of Created Works

Titles of created works like books, movies, or newspaper articles, should have first, last, and all main words in between capitalized.

Toni Morrison was a single mother when she began writing her novel *The Bluest Eye*.

In the early 1950s, artist Helen Frankenthaler created a new type of art when she used poured paint instead of brushes in her work *Mountains and Sea*.

A *New York Times* critic wrote in 1987 that *I Love Lucy* "is a cultural fact of life."

Minor words in a title are generally not capitalized unless they come first or last in the title, or follow a colon. Minor words include articles (*a, an, the*), conjunctions (*and, but, for, or, nor, so, yet*), and prepositions (such as *in, on, at, of, from*).

- *Indiana Jones and the Temple of Doom*
- *The Hobbit: An Unexpected Journey*
- *Captain America: The Winter Soldier*

Quotations

The first letter of a quoted sentence should be capitalized.

On the subject of the weather, Mark Twain said, "It is best to read the weather forecast before we pray for rain."

Only the first word of a quoted sentence is capitalized, even when you break the sentence with your own words.

"*The* proper office of a friend," Mark Twain wrote in his notebook, "*is* to side with you when you are in the wrong. *Nearly* anybody will side with you when you are in the right."

When a quote is longer than one sentence, each sentence should begin with a capital letter.

"*He* was ignorant of the commonest accomplishments of youth," said Mark Twain of George Washington. "*He* would not even lie."

18.2 Spelling

The two easiest ways to improve your spelling are to read a lot and to use a dictionary when you're uncertain. Whether online or in print, the dictionary is much more reliable than computer and smartphone spell-checking functions, which often miss homophone errors (two words that sound alike).

Homophones

See if you can spot what's wrong with the following sentence.

Today, when tourists flock to Abbey Road studios, there probably aware that the Beatles made they're famous album their in 1969.

Were you confused by the misspelled *homophones*? A *homophone* is a word that sounds like another word but is spelled differently. Below are the homophones correctly placed.

Today, when tourists flock to Abbey Road studios, *they're* probably aware that the Beatles made *their* famous album *there* in 1968.

Here are some other commonly misspelled homophones.

accept/except

> He *accepted* all of the awards *except* the lifetime achievement award, which he insisted should go to his mentor.

affect/effect

Perhaps the trickiest of all homophones.
Generally, *affect* is used as a verb, and *effect* is used as a noun.

> The golfer leaned to try to *affect* the flight of the ball, but his body language had no *effect*.

lead/led

> The tour guide *led* us to the entrance of the *lead* mine, but we weren't allowed in.

lessen/lesson

> The physics *lesson* was on how opposite forces *lessen* velocity.

sole/soul

> The *sole* job of a good poet is to lay bare the human *soul*.

stationary/stationery

> Janice perfected her calligraphy technique by writing on *stationery* while riding on her *stationary* bike.

then/than

> *Then* there was nothing left to say other *than* "thank you."

too/to/two

> The *two* hikers were traveling *to* Brixton *too*, so we gave them a ride.

weather/whether

> We checked the news to see *whether* the *weather* would be nice for the beach.

weight/wait

> The *weight*lifter *waited* for his partner to add more *weight* for the next set.

who's/whose

> Ahmed texted to see *whose* car we are taking and *who's* driving.

you're/your

> *You're* the only one who can plan *your* schedule.

Commonly Misspelled Words

One way to improve your spelling is just to be aware of which words tend to be challenging. Here are some more commonly misspelled words for you to review.

accommodate

achieve

across

apparently

argument

assassination

believe

bizarre

business

calendar

Caribbean

committee

conscious

curiosity

definitely

disappear

embarrass

foreign

government

guard

humorous

incidentally

independent

interrupt

irresistible

knowledge

millennium, millennia

necessary

noticeable

occasion

occurred, occurring, occurrence

persistent

pharaoh

politician

preferred, preferring

really

referred, referring

resistance

separate

successful

supersede

surprise

therefore

threshold

tomorrow

truly

unfortunately

18.3 Vocabulary and Word Roots

If your parents asked you to consent to a nonsensical plan to wake up everybody in the house with a light-sensor alarm clock, would you resent it, or would you be too sentimental to object?

The above sentence may not make much sense, except as an illustration of how word roots connect many words with related meanings. How many words in the preceding two sentences have as their basis the Latin root *sent* or *sens*, meaning "to feel"?

A *root* is the origin of a word, often from a different language. Recognizing the roots of words can help you understand their meanings. The words *consent, nonsensical, sensor, resent, sentimental, sentence,* and *sense* may all be familiar to you. But the root, meaning "to feel," might help you understand the meaning of an unfamiliar word, like *sentient*.

Many roots form new words by adding *prefixes* and/or *suffixes* to the root. The addition of the prefix *in-* and the suffix *-itive* turn the root *sens* into the word *insensitive*.

Below are some common roots, their meanings, and words derived from these roots.

ROOT	MEANING	WORDS
-audi- (Latin)	to hear	audible, auditory, audiovisual
-bene- (Greek)	good, well	benevolent, beneficial, benefit
-bio- (Greek)	life	biology, autobiography, biotech
-duc(t)- (Latin)	to lead, to make	conduct, education, induce
-gen- (Greek)	race, kind	genetic, regenerate, genre
-geo- (Greek)	earth	geography, geode, geometry
-graph- (Greek)	to write	graphite, autograph, paragraph
-jur-, -jus- (Latin)	law	injustice, jury, jurisdiction
-log(o)- (Greek)	word, thought	logical, sociology, dialogue
-luc- (Latin)	light	translucent, elucidate, lucid
-manu- (Latin)	hand	manuscript, manual, manufacture
-mit-, -mis- (Latin)	to send	transmit, mission, permission
-path- (Greek)	feel, suffer	sympathy, telepathy, pathos
-phil- (Greek)	love	philosophy, Francophile, philanthropy
-photo- (Greek)	light	photosynthesis, photocopy, telephoto
-port- (Latin)	to carry	transportation, portable, important
-psych- (Greek)	soul	psyche, psychiatry, psychic
-scrib-, -script- (Latin)	to write	transcription, scripture, unscripted
-sent-, -sens- (Latin)	to feel	sensitive, consensual, sentient
-tele- (Greek)	far away	television, telekinesis, telepathy
-tend- (Latin)	to stretch	extend, contending, distended
-terr- (Latin)	earth	terrain, extraterrestrial, disinter
-vac- (Latin)	empty	vacuum, vacation, vacuous
-vid-, -vis- (Latin)	to see	invisible, video, visor

Sample Student Papers

This appendix features two sample student research papers in the MLA format. One addresses the costs of higher education, and the other looks at the effects of "fake news" in recent years. Your assignments may strike a different balance between research and various rhetorical modes, but these sample papers can serve as effective models as you work on your own writing. Discussion questions follow each paper.

Eliza Dowery
Professor Mandell
Composition I
October 22, 2022

The Cost of Higher Education in More Ways Than One

More than credit card debt and car payments, Americans are drowning in student loan debt. In 2018, Americans had about 1.5 *trillion* total dollars of student loan debt—around thirty thousand dollars per person (Heuvel). This number has been high for years and has prompted many to wonder if there is a better system that could ease the burden on those who wish to continue their education. After all, in many other nations, college is either much less expensive or, in some cases, virtually free. For example, the average cost of a year's tuition at a public university in Switzerland is about $1,000, compared to $8,000 in the United States and nearly $12,000 in the United Kingdom (Gellerman). Scholars and economists have suggested many ways to lessen the cost of higher education, and each possible solution has benefits and drawbacks. What is clear, however, is that this massive accumulation of debt cannot go on forever. To solve these problems, it would make sense to make a college education free for those who truly need it.

According to Natalia Abrams, executive director of Student Debt Crisis, an organization devoted to reforming student debt policies, student debt has had "a disastrous domino effect for millions of Americans." She goes on to say the following:

> The reality of the day-to-day crisis is staggering. The average borrower has under $1,000 in savings, and 80% cannot save for retirement. And we are not just talking young people — we've talked to many borrowers in their sixties who are still trying to pay off their student loans and are worried they will never have enough to retire. (qtd in Hembree)

As Elyssa Kirkham points out, large amounts of debt can slow the growth of new businesses, lower the rate of homeownership, and weaken consumer spending. If people are paying off their large student loans, they have less to spend in areas that make the economy run: goods and services, new businesses, and property. Student debt even can stop people from getting married and having children, which can also negatively affect the economy (Kirkham). In addition, it is low- and middle-income people who are most likely to take out loans, which increases income inequality (Hembree).

Many proposals have been made to address this problem. Some suggest increasing financial aid to those who need it or forgiving student loan debt entirely. Others believe that the answer can be found by reforming college itself. These proponents of free college advocate scrapping the current higher education model and moving toward a new system that would not require students to pay tuition. Some countries have implemented this method, with varying degrees of success. Scholars have analyzed these countries and their programs, finding that like most things, free college comes with both positive and negative effects.

Implementing a free college program can have many beneficial outcomes. In a small-scale application of "free college," the University of Michigan promised highly qualified, low-income students that if they were accepted into the university, they could attend free. This led to many more low-income students applying and enrolling at the school. If not for this program, a lot of the students who were accepted would not have even applied to college. As *The Atlantic* reporter Adam Harris observes, "Many high-achieving students from a low-income or minority background don't think they can get in to a prestigious institution, let alone pay for it — despite the fact that many such colleges have generous financial-aid packages — so they end up not applying." This pilot implementation of free college suggests that if such a program were implemented across the state or the nation, the effects on low-income and minority students would be similar: they would pursue higher education at increased rates.

Why is it important that more people attend college? On an individual level, having a college degree has a significant impact on a person's quality of life. David J. Deming points out that "looking beyond earnings, all of today's most pressing social problems — from declining male labor force participation to falling marriage rates and increases in single parenthood to rising mortality and opioid addiction — disproportionately afflict people without college degrees." (2). The benefits go well beyond individual growth and security, however. Having a more educated population results in a dramatic increase in the quality and economic health of a community. A well-educated population experiences "less unemployment, reduced dependence on public assistance programs, and greater tax revenue. Education also plays a key role in the reduction of crime, improved public health, and greater political and civic engagement" (Mitra 5). In other words, the benefits of education go far beyond the individual, positively affecting society as a whole.

Free college might also help equalize the experience of wealthy and low-income students. Although the university is supposed to provide an equal playing field for everyone regardless of background, this is not how it usually works. Anthony Abraham Jack, now a professor at Harvard's Graduate School of Education, remembers his time as a first-generation, low-income student: he had to work long hours to send money back home to his family and often went hungry when campus dining was closed. He writes that his "financial-aid officer didn't understand why I worked so many jobs or why I picked up even more hours at times." The university simply was not equipped to accommodate his needs, which are similar to the needs of many low-income and first-generation students today. Although Professor Jack ended up excelling in college and obtaining his Ph.D., that is not the reality for many students in his situation. Clearly, making college free would help these students.

Free college would also enable students from low-income families to concentrate on their studies. As Anthony P. Carnevale argues, "Working while learning takes a greater toll on low-income students. [...] These working learners are more likely than their higher-income peers to work more than 15 hours per week, leaving less time for their studies." Because low-income students might have less time for educational pursuits, they often earn an average of C or lower. They are also less likely to graduate on time because work interferes with their ability to take more classes per semester (Carnevale). Free college programs would ease the burden on low-income students, who would not have to work while in school to pay their tuition. By equalizing the amount of time low-income students spend on their studies in comparison to their wealthier peers, free college could level the playing field for students of all backgrounds.

While free college may seem to be an ideal solution, it has some drawbacks. One of the most common objections to its implementation is the cost. For example, Germany has gradually eliminated tuition for its public universities, and now students only have to pay just a few hundred euros a year for administrative fees. Although enrollment has soared by 22 percent, the taxpayer cost of subsidizing higher education increased by 37 percent. As Jon Marcus observes, without tuition revenue, universities will suffer. In addition, "Economists wonder how long the government will be able to support these costs." Unfortunately, free college is not really free. It takes revenue, usually a great deal of it, from limited sources, to fund this program. In addition, Germany's free college program does not help students with living expenses. Even if they do not have to pay tuition, some students still have to work to cover rent and other expenses (Marcus).

Another potential problem of free college is overcrowding. If college is free, and there is no barrier to attending, prospective students will apply at higher rates. This will cause the opposite of what free college was meant to do: make higher education more accessible to all. A Georgetown study of one free college plan foresaw a possible negative outcome:

> [So] many people in the United States would apply to go to top public universities that those would become much more selective, shutting out poor and nonwhite students, who would land in already overburdened open-access regional public universities and community colleges with low success rates. (Marcus)

If the resources and spots open for students are the same but many more people apply, a university will have no choice but to become more selective and possibly exacerbate the disparities that already exist. For example, due to a lack of funding for qualified teachers, students at some German universities attend overcrowded lectures and are taught by underpaid Ph.Ds. or even undergraduates (Marcus).

Although the arguments both for and against free college are compelling, working toward a more affordable higher education system is necessary as student debt becomes a heavier and heavier burden. By learning from the successes and failures of other free college programs, including those implemented in other countries, educators and administrators can devise a new and better system. An ideal free college policy would eliminate tuition for those who need it while providing living expenses and other costs for low-income students. In order to reduce the cost to taxpayers, this free college program could still require tuition from wealthier students, who would not be unduly burdened by debt. This sliding scale would break down barriers of race and class that currently plague the university system. Free college certainly wouldn't solve all the issues facing American higher education, but it would go a long way toward fulfilling the promise of America by giving all students the opportunity to realize their full potential.

Works Cited

Carnevale, Anthony P. "Working While in College Might Hurt Students More Than It Helps." *CNBC*, 24 Oct. 2019. *www.cnbc.com*, www.cnbc.com/2019/10/24/working-in-college-can-hurt-low-income-students-more-than-help.html.

Deming, David J. "The Economics of Free College." *Economics for Inclusive Prosperity*. econfip.org, econfip.org/policy-brief/the-economics-of-free-college/. Accessed 30 Mar. 2020.

Gellerman, Erica. "What Does College Cost Around the World?" *Earnest*, 10 July 2019. *www.earnest.com*, www.earnest.com/blog/college-costs-around-the-world/.

Harris, Adam. "A Guarantee of Tuition-Free College Can Have Life-Changing Effects." *Atlantic*, 11 Dec. 2018. www.theatlantic.com/education/archive/2018/12/life-changing-effects-free-college/577831/.

Hembree, Diana. "New Report Finds Student Debt Burden Has 'Disastrous Domino Effect' on Millions of Americans." *Forbes*, 1 Nov. 2018. *www.forbes.com*, www.forbes.com/sites/dianahembree/2018/11/01/new-report-finds-student-debt

-burden-has-disastrous-domino-effect-on-millions-of-americans/.
Accessed 11 Apr. 2020.

Heuvel, Katrina vanden. "Americans Are Drowning in Student-Loan
Debt. The US Should Forgive All of It." *Nation*, June 2018.
www.thenation.com/article/archive/americans-drowning
-student-loan-debt-us-forgive/.

Jack, Anthony Abraham. "I Was a Low-Income College Student.
Classes Weren't the Hard Part." *New York Times*, 10 Sept. 2019.
www.nytimes.com/interactive/2019/09/10/magazine/college
-inequality.html.

Kirkham, Elyssa. "What Are the Effects of Student Loan Debt on the
Economy?" *Student Loan Hero*, 28 Oct. 2019. studentloanhero
.com/featured/effects-of-student-loan-debt-us-economy/.

Marcus, Jon. "How Free College Tuition in One Country Exposes
Unexpected Pros and Cons." *Hechinger Report*, 18 Oct. 2016.
hechingerreport.org, hechingerreport.org/free-college-tuition
-one-country-exposes-unexpected-pros-cons/.

Mitra, Dana. *Pennsylvania's Best Investment: The Social and
Economic Benefits of Public Education.* www.elc-pa.org/wp
-content/uploads/2011/06/BestInvestment_Full_Report
_6.27.11.pdf. Accessed 30 Mar. 2020.

Discussion Questions

1. What evidence does the author provide to support her argument that
   eliminating college tuition is the best solution for the student-loan debt
   crisis, and how well does that evidence support her argument?

2. How appropriate is the paper's title, which implies that student-loan
   debt has an impact that goes beyond just economic. Does its content
   explain what those additional costs are?

3. The author assumes that the audience agrees with her belief that
   everyone deserves the same opportunity to go to college. Was this a safe
   assumption? Do most people believe that life should be fair or that creating an "equal playing field" is beneficial to society?

4. When the author points out that free college isn't actually free, what
   does she mean?

5. The argument for free college implies that cost is the biggest hurdle
   students must overcome. Do you agree? What are some of the other
   obstacles students must overcome and how do they rank in order of
   importance?

Rami Khan

Professor Kirszner

Composition I

5 February 2023

What Is "Fake News" — and Why Is It Our Problem?

We are all familiar with the term "fake news," but do we know what it actually means or where it originated? It is now nearly impossible to hear the term and not think of President Trump's use of it, but the two words simply denote deliberately false information. In a press conference in 2019, Donald Trump claimed that he coined the term "fake news." This statement was, in itself, fake news, as the term had actually been popularized by BuzzFeed news media editor Craig Silverman in 2014 (Beaujon). Regardless of when and where the term originated, fake news is actually being accepted and normalized due to social media, and this trend has potentially dangerous ramifications.

The practice of spreading misinformation is as old as human civilization itself. In her essay "History of Fake News," Joanna M. Burkhardt suggests that "[the control of information] has probably contributed to the creation of most of the hierarchical cultures we know today" (5). She argues that in early civilizations, kings, queens, and religious leaders were the only individuals with access to written information. As a result, misinformation could be used to win the favor of those in power — or those in power could choose which information to reveal to their illiterate subjects.

With the invention of the printing press, however, literacy spread, and suddenly written information (both true and false) could be used to influence many people in a short span of time. As technology advanced, so too did the ability to spread information to the masses. The invention of the telegraph and the telephone allowed for knowledge to be transferred faster than ever before, and the widespread integration of the radio into everyday life in the twentieth century made it easy for large groups of people to receive information in real time.

While the potential for spreading accurate information developed alongside these technological advances, so too did the reach of fake news. One example was Orson Welles's infamous 1938 *The War of the Worlds* radio broadcast. In this Halloween special on CBS, Welles and his team adapted a classic science-fiction novel about aliens invading Earth into a fictional radiobroadcast.

Actors read "news flashes" about an alien invasion, and although
disclaimers at the beginning and during the broadcast explained that
the information was fictitious, many listeners took the broadcast
to be true. This led to mass hysteria across the country. At a press
conference the next day, Welles denied that he had intentionally
deceived audiences. However, according to A. Brad Schwartz, "Hardly
anyone, then or since, has taken [Welles] at his word" (Schwartz).
Welles used his overnight notoriety to launch a successful Hollywood
career, leading many to speculate that the entire stunt was for
Welles's personal gain. In later years, however, he often claimed that
"[his company] had always hoped to fool some of their listeners,
in order to teach them a lesson about not believing whatever they
heard on the radio" (Schwartz). This broadcast is a well-documented
instance of hordes of people willing to believe anything without
looking into the source.

Since Welles's time, we have experienced many technological
advances that have helped to blur the line between news and
entertainment. Television, for example, was initially seen as a
vehicle for entertainment, until broadcast companies realized it had
journalistic potential. In the 1960s and 70s, coverage of the Vietnam
War was beamed directly into living rooms as it was broadcast on
television. Viewers could now watch graphic war footage before
switching over to their favorite variety show.

In the twenty-first century, the most prevalent technology
for sharing and accessing information is the Internet, and here
the line between entertainment and legitimate news is less
distinct than ever before. Instead of getting a printed newspaper,
people can easily go to the publication's website and get the same
information. Rather than tune in to the news on TV, people can
conveniently look the broadcast up on free video-sharing websites
like YouTube. Or, they can avoid all of that, and simply scroll
through social media and get the news there. According to a 2019
study cited by *MIS Quarterly*, more than 50% of American adults
read news on social media.

This situation in itself is not necessarily a problem; as
technology changes, so does the way people consume it. What
is troubling is this: "Social media is different from other media
providing news ... because users do not choose the source of
all the articles they see on social media. Instead, proprietary
algorithms provide targeted information with little transparency"

(Moravec et. al. 1344). In 2011, tech entrepreneur Eli Pariser gave a TED Talk in which he coined the phrase "filter bubble" to refer to an individual's personal page on popular social media websites like Facebook and Twitter. As Pariser explains, there is so much raw information on the Internet that a series of algorithms filter out content that they deem irrelevant and filter *in* content they believe will entertain the reader. These algorithms determine what to show based on everything about a user's online profile: political views, friends' political views, profession, location, favorite movies, and so on. As Pariser notes, "What's in your filter bubble depends on who you are, and it depends on what you do. But the thing is that you don't decide what gets in. And more importantly, you don't actually see what gets edited out." In other words, although people may consume news on social media with the intention of staying informed, they are actually getting a view of the world that is curated to match their preexisting beliefs.

Another factor that encourages the dissemination of fake news is conformation bias. The American Psychological Association defines the term "confirmation bias" as "the tendency to gather evidence that confirms preexisting expectations, typically by emphasizing or pursuing supporting evidence while dismissing or failing to seek contradictory evidence." This phenomenon is precisely what social media encourages and is, in fact, the principal attraction for many users. In 2019, *MIS Quarterly* published a study in which researchers recorded electrical patterns of the brain while their subjects engaged with social media. Their findings supported the strength of confirmation bias:

> [A]rticles that aligned with the users' a priori opinions triggered increased cognitive activity, with users more likely to believe them; articles that challenged users' opinions were less thoroughly considered and were less likely to be believed.... The hedonic mindset when reading social media news means the user's goal is not to determine what is true and fake; instead the goal is enjoyment and pleasure.... Users engage with articles that make them feel good, which tend to be articles supporting their beliefs. (Moravec et. al. 1344)

This study demonstrates that people's brains are not primed to think critically when engaging with social media. Instead, people log on to be entertained, and they mentally process news articles in the same way they process entertainment. Users tend to dismiss articles that are upsetting or run counter to their beliefs, regardless of the validity of the information.

Part of the reason fake news is so pervasive on social media is that users are apathetic about sharing it. In a 2019 psychological study, researchers found that "seeing a fake-news headline one to four times reduced how unethical participants thought it was to publish and share that headline when they saw it again — even when it was clearly labeled as false and participants disbelieved it...." (Effron and Raj 75). This is hardly the only study to explore why the spread of fake news is so prolific. A 2016 study measuring what people were actually clicking on and engaging with on Twitter found that more than half of the articles shared and/or reposted were sent without the user's actually reading beyond the headline (Gabielkov et. al.). In other words, people share false information — often without even reading it — and many do not think that there is anything ethically wrong with doing this. Despite how frequently politicians and media personalities proclaim that fake news is a problem, everyday citizens are the ones who normalize the spread of it through the use of social media.

If people are aware that fake news proliferates online and the practice is widely accepted as a consequence of the information age, is there really a problem? It is easy to convince ourselves that fake news stays in the online sphere, that whatever is happening in the virtual world has no bearing on reality, and that fake news amounts to no more than tabloid gossip. But the "real world" results of fake news have already had a very real (and negative) impact on modern society.

In the wake of the 2016 presidential election, Facebook came under severe scrutiny after it was revealed that fake Russian accounts had purchased roughly $100,000 in targeted political ads. "The full effect of these ads is not yet known, but it has been established that these ads reached many people and may indeed may have influenced their thinking and opinions, particularly if people did not realize that the information presented in the ads was fake" (Cooke 4). Never in the history of the United States have foreign powers had such easy access to the minds of American citizens as they do in the Internet age. Now more than ever, hostile countries can try to manipulate American citizens, and the citizens themselves can unwittingly become responsible for the sharing and acceptance of potentially dangerous propaganda. What is at stake is the very sanctity of American democracy through the absent-minded sharing of fake and deliberately malicious propaganda wedged between the newest music video and a funny cat meme.

Although "fake news" has been around for a long time, never before have citizens been so complicit in obfuscating facts through the spread of propaganda. What this means is that they legitimize fake news by circulating it alongside truthful, factual information. It is up to us, the major consumers and disseminators of fake news, as well as the major news outlets, to do something about it. Specifically, it is the responsibility of social media users, public figures, and journalists to think critically about whether something is true, or whether it is just entertainment.

Works Cited

Burkhardt, Joanna M. "History of Fake News." *Library Technology Reports*, vol. 53.8 (2017): 5–8.

"confirmation bias." *APA*, dictionary.apa.org/confirmation-bias.

Cooke, Nicole A. *Fake News and Alternative Facts: Information Literacy in a Post-Truth Era*. American Library Association, 2018.

Effron, Daniel A., and Medha Raj. "Misinformation and Morality: Encountering Fake-News Headlines Makes Them Seem Less Unethical to Publish and Share." *Association for Psychological Science* 31.1 (2020): 75–87.

Gabielkov, M., A. Ramachandran, A. Chaintreau, and A. Legout. 2016. "Social Clicks: What and Who Gets Read on Twitter?" ACM SIGMETRICS/IFIP Performance, Antibes Juan-les-Pins, France. June 2016.

Moravec, Patricia L., et. al. "Fake News on Social Media: People Believe What They Want to Believe Even When It Makes No Sense at All." *MIS Quarterly* 43.4 (2019): 1343–60.

Pariser, Eli. "Beware Online 'Filter Bubbles.'" *TED: Ideas Worth Spreading*. May 2011, www.ted.com/talks/eli_pariser_beware _online_filter_bubbles.

@realDonaldTrump. "So much FAKE NEWS!" *Twitter*, 9 Mar. 2020, 9:17 a.m., twitter.com/realDonaldTrump /status/1237004509156642816.

Schwartz, Brad A. "The Infamous 'War of the Worlds' Radio Broadcast Was a Magnificent Fluke." *Smithsonian Magazine*, 6 May 2015, www.smithsonianmag.com/history/infamous-war-worlds-radio -broadcast-was-magnificent-fluke-180955180/.

Discussion Questions

1. Both the title and thesis statement of this essay imply that "fake news" has detrimental consequences. What examples does the author provide to support this claim and how effective are they?

2. This paper shows how individual bias affects the proliferation of fake news. Do you see any diction or assertions that might reveal the author's own bias?

3. As the author points out, people on social media are more likely to read, enjoy, and share information that affirms their beliefs. If people were more aware of this tendency, do you think they would try harder to verify information's veracity before sharing it? How diligent are you in verifying the accuracy of information you share?

4. According to the author, social media companies use technology to make certain their consumers are entertained rather than informed. Do you consider this tactic immoral, and if so, should it be made illegal? Why or why not? Before you answer, consider all the businesses that produce products that are hazardous to the public.

INDEX